Dear S,

It was truly a joy to have you here today. Many blessings

Lorri

My Father the Fish

Rendering Life's Hardships Spiritual: A Memoir

My Father the Fish

Rendering Life's Hardships
Spiritual: A Memoir

by
Lorri Danzig

Copyright © 2019 by Lorri Danzig
All rights reserved. No part of this book may be reproduced,
scanned, or distributed in any printed or electronic form
without permission of the author.
First Edition: June 2019
Printed in the United States of America
ISBN 13: 978-1-64550-272-2

For Andy, my *beshert*, without whose love and support this book would not have come to be.

Acknowledgement

This book is dedicated with gratitude to Dr. Joseph Piepmeier, Dr. Veronica Marer, Dr. Patricia Fountain, the entire team of doctors, nurses, orderlies and other staff of Yale New Haven Hospital who played a role in my medical treatment and recovery, Rabbi Adam Haston who organized the wondrous team of helping hands who cooked meals, ran errands, and chauffeured me, Cheryl and Joel Gelernter who took me for a walk, Igor and Nina Yukov who showed me the power of prayer, Reva Danzig who saw to intimate details of my post-op care with presence and a tender touch, David Danzig who prepped me for surgery with skillful woo-woo, Debbie Danzig-Brodie who offered the comforting and caring presence of a skilled nurse, Juliet and Selig Danzig for always supporting me, Matt Hochman, who is there for me when I need him, my mother, Beverly Hochman whose wise words helped get me through, and Dr. Robert C. Sohn, my Gurudev, who gave me the tools to see the world in a new way and empowered me on this journey.

Author's Note

I am a student of spiritual work. This book recalls one year in my journey. Like a snapshot, it faithfully reflects my thought process and understanding at that time. I understand many things differently today. I see through a clearer lens. This is as it should be. Spiritual work is a process. There is no standing still. If understanding does not evolve, it inevitably diminishes.

Finally, this book is a work of nonfiction. None of the events are invented, and I have been faithful to the truth as I remember it. In keeping with the maxim to do no harm, the name, Dr. Gardiner, is a pseudonym.

If you look at the world in a new way, you will see a new world, and you will be a new part of that new world.

—Robert C. Sohn

Lorri Danzig

Part One

Lorri Danzig

One

By the time I pulled onto the Merritt Parkway it was already dark. I squinted in the glare of the oncoming headlights, leaning into the steering wheel and straining to bring the road into focus. I didn't like driving at night. The familiar voices of NPR droned from the radio and I was beginning to relax when the world beyond my windshield went flat. Just like that, in an instant. Cars, guardrails, road signs all steam-rolled. Three dimensions pan-caked into two. I had stumbled into Flatland. Like Alice tumbling down the rabbit hole, I was curious but not alarmed, and this was even have a tendency to operate in overdrive, were comfortably coasting in cruise control.

My car barreled toward the exit for the Hamden Library. As I approached the ramp, a wide black brushstroke bisecting the grassy shoulder, I expected a corridor which should lead from here to there. But I detected no there as distinct from here: no foreground, no off-in-the-distance. To veer onto the ramp was to travel in a direction that appeared non-existent. The car ahead of me was signaling right. My eyes glued to its taillights, I took a deep breath and followed it.

Once off the highway, I didn't pull over. I was on the way to a meeting that was important to me, and scrapping my plan wasn't an option I considered. I told myself my night vision must be deteriorating and I would have to make an appointment with the eye doctor to get it checked out. I wondered if the vision problem could even be a symptom of menopause. I was fifty-four, and over the past few years I had come to think of almost any aberration from the normal as possibly connected to the change of life. Night sweats,

3

insomnia, frequent peeing, dry skin? All menopause. Annoying, yes, but not anything to panic about.

Once I'd exited onto city streets, the highway vista was replaced by a suburban commercial strip—also flat. I knew the entrance to the library parking lot was very close, and though my eyes could see the break where the driveway crossed the sidewalk, I could not conceive of a way to execute the necessary left-hand turn. I drove on and on into a seedy section of town. The streets were deserted. Some windows were boarded up, others barred. A scruffy group of men slumped against the wall in front of a bar. I was terrified of getting stuck there. I had to find a way to turn the car around so I could head back in the direction of the library.

When I was a kid, Sunday was family day. We had often made the trip from Long Island into Manhattan to visit the Museum of Natural History or to see a matinee on Broadway. My dad would take the Queens-Midtown Tunnel into the city. As we approached the mouth of the tunnel, no matter how hot it was, he would tell us to roll up the windows. There was always heavy traffic there and for minutes at a time we'd be at a standstill. Men, unshaven and disheveled, would stagger over to the car and wipe the windshield with their grimy rags then rap on my dad's window with one hand, holding out the other, palm up. I was a well-scrubbed, middle-class kid from the suburbs who knew nothing of homelessness or urban poverty. This onslaught by down-and-out strangers had terrified me, and it was this memory that surfaced as I struggled to navigate the streets of Hamden.

Up ahead, I saw a strip mall. Holding my breath I aimed for the entrance to its parking lot. I attempted the turn with fluttering fear and lingering doubts like those of a first-time skydiver who flicks his eyes toward his chute cord as he bails from the plane. Once off the road, I brought the car to a full stop, shifted into park, and pressed my forehead against the steering wheel. My heart pounded. Relieved to be at a standstill, I would have liked to stay that way, but I was determined to get to the meeting.

I sat for several minutes while my breathing regulated then pulled out of the lot and drove toward the library. I should have realized it was reckless to continue on, but I didn't. I felt brave, powerful, and resourceful, more than capable of overcoming the fear that pounded in my chest. By the time I arrived, my meeting had started, and my perceptions had returned to normal.

Over the next few hours, I channel-surfed between two worlds as the weirdness came and went. When I found myself in Flatland, I was removed from the scene as though I were on the darkened side of a one-way mirror. My cardboard colleagues sat around the table with their paper doll hands scribbling on notepads or plastered to Styrofoam coffee cups. Despite my feeling not all there, I was given no reason to suspect my comments were anything less than coherent or my behavior other than normal. No one appeared to take particular notice of me. Midway into the meeting, I left to go to the restroom on the first floor. I felt as though I was floating down the wide, open staircase. I surveyed the patrons below as they wandered through the stacks. Alighting on the ground floor, I headed toward the information desk and asked directions to the ladies' room. I was vaguely aware that I had understood and yet had not understood the librarian's words. In the end, I took off in the direction in which she had pointed.

I moved like a dreamer. In the lavatory, the ceiling and floor, walls and fixtures were a disorienting uniform white. I staggered into a stall, pulled down my pants, and squatted. I couldn't judge the distance to the bowl and wasn't sure how to aim into it. I did the best I could and then struggled with my zipper and with the sliding latch on the metal door. I stumbled when it swung open and deposited me back into the larger white on white chamber. I wanted to get back to the meeting, and I willed my body to keep moving, but my legs did not respond. Minutes passed. I stood there, a statue watching my reflection in the mirror. I was aware of two distinct layers of emotion. I was serene, at peace with the stillness, and at the same time anxiety hopped within my chest like a flea on a dog's ear. I waited. After three minutes, maybe five, the door to the ladies' room opened. The movement reflected in the mirror thawed my frozen legs. Reactivated, they hurried me out of the bathroom and back to the meeting.

The rest of the evening brought more of the same: intervals of normalcy punctuated by periodic stops. My life was progressing at the whim of a projectionist who from time to time chose to pause the film. Yet the projector's bulb, like the light of consciousness, never ceased to burn bright.

Over the course of the evening, I considered various diagnoses ranging from chemical imbalance to low blood sugar to hormones out of whack. But I could come up with no explanation for the perceived flatness and loss of movement. Still, I assured myself whatever the cause, it couldn't be serious. Like Scarlett O'Hara, I couldn't bear to think too much about it then; I would think about it tomorrow.

At the end of the meeting, I once again floated down the stairs. I headed towards the illuminated exit signs above the main doors. I was altogether uncertain how I would get through, but they opened automatically as I drew near. My disobedient legs carried me out to the library parking lot in a staccato pattern of stop-start, stop-start. I lurched forward like a mechanical doll with a loose wire. For several minutes I stood stock still staring out into the semi-darkness until my car drifted into focus. The jolt of recognition jump-started my own internal battery and set my legs back in motion.

I stood beside my car, fumbling with my keys, not quite sure what to do with them. A black man, twenty something, in a knitted ski hat and leather jacket approached. The hair stood up on my neck as I scanned the deserted parking lot. I couldn't move. I gripped my keys like a weapon, and I waited. "Ma'am," he said. "You just getting here? 'Cause the library's closed. It's after nine."

I managed a nod and a faint smile as the terror drained from my face leaving me feeling embarrassed. I knew if he had been older and dressed in a suit and tie or even young, but white, I would not have reacted the way I had.

Please, I tried to call out as he turned to walk away. *I need help*. But my lips never moved. *Where are my words?* I despaired as I watched him get in his car and drive off.

I returned my attention to unlocking the car. One by one, I held the keys up to the lock, but I didn't try to insert any of them. I fingered the wireless key fobs on my chain—one for my husband's car, one for mine—and pushed each of the buttons in turn until I heard the click. I pressed into and then finally squeezed on the door handle, swinging the door open and collapsing onto the driver's seat. I started the engine, peered out the window at the parking lot exit, and studied the directions to the library that still lay on the seat. I visualized both the route home and the steps necessary to put the car in gear, but I could not fathom how to execute the steps. The messages issued by my command center were not reaching their destination in my limbs. My ears perked at the drone of the engine. Remembering the car was running, I began to sweat. The windows were shut tight against the bite of December cold, and the parking lot was dimly lit and almost empty. Would I be trapped here overnight? Would I asphyxiate or freeze? Both felt like real possibilities, and the anticipation set off an alarm in me that should have sounded hours before.

The clock on my dashboard read 9:05 p.m. Soon, the very last car would leave the parking lot. I had to get help and quickly. But turning off the engine and getting out of the car proved even more difficult than getting in had been. I stabbed at the ignition key and tried to curl my clumsy gloved

7

fingers around it. After many attempts, I managed to shut off the engine. Unbuckling my seatbelt and pulling up on the door handle was nearly impossible; my hands fumbled, thrust, and jabbed. When I finally heard the catch release, I leaned into the door, swung my feet out of the car, and pulled myself up and out. Under my weight, the door slammed closed. Through the window I saw my pocketbook sitting on the seat. It contained both my wallet and phone. If I fell or passed out no one would be able to identify me, but I didn't even try to get the door open again. I knew I couldn't do it.

Lights still shone through the library windows. I managed several steps in that direction before my legs quit walking again, stranding me, a boat adrift in a blacktop sea. And then, walking toward me, I saw a woman in a pea coat and dark skirt holding a little girl by her white-mittened hand.

"You've been standing here quite a while," the woman said. "You look confused. Are you okay?"

I considered her question and hoped this time I could push the words past my lips. "No," I said. "I don't know how to work my car."

It didn't occur to me this woman might have found my statement odd. She didn't ask how I'd gotten there or if the car keys I held were even mine. She took me by the arm and guided me toward the library.

"Let's get you inside," she said. I told her I had come from a meeting on the second floor, and she delivered me there, leaving me in the company of several stragglers from the group who were chatting with each other.

Dana was among them. I knew her, though not well. We had met a couple of years earlier and I ran into her at meetings in the community on occasion. I remembered she was a nurse and so I turned to her.

"Excuse me," I said, interrupting their chatter.

All the women turned to me. I focused my eyes on Dana and gave a brief retelling of my experiences that evening.

"And so," I concluded, "I couldn't figure out how to

drive the car. But I think I'm okay now."

Dana was calm and direct.

"That may be," she said. "But there is no way you should get back behind the wheel. You need to get checked out by a doctor."

Two of the other women offered to get me home, and I accepted, relieved not to have to deal with my car any longer.

Dana asked if my husband was home and then asked for the number. She called and told him I wasn't feeling well and that someone was bringing me home. It didn't occur to me to speak to Andy myself.

"She should see a doctor," I heard Dana tell him. But by this time my ability to walk and talk had returned, and I discounted her words.

Much ado about nothing, I thought, as I again latched onto an earlier self-diagnosis: low blood sugar. I handed my keys to the tall woman who had offered to drive my car and followed the other, a heavyset lady, to hers. Though I felt grateful for the rescue, I was more than a little embarrassed.

♦♦♦

Construction on the Merritt Parkway made the ride home slow going. My driver kept glancing over in my direction. I fixed my eyes on the dashboard. I was seeing flat again, and the scenery passing outside the window made me dizzy. I wondered if she could tell. As we approached the next exit she suggested maybe we'd made a mistake and should have gone straight to an emergency room. She wanted to get off the highway and head for a hospital, but I assured her it wasn't necessary, I was fine. In truth, I felt altogether not fine, but if I could convince her otherwise I thought maybe it would be so.

Andy must have heard the two-car caravan pull into our driveway. He came out to meet us. His black leather bomber jacket was unzipped. His *kippah* sat askew atop his head of unruly black hair and his *tsitsis*, ritual prayer fringes, swung at his sides. He didn't look concerned. Dana had said only that I wasn't feeling well, and he was not one to get excited over physical ailments. He tended to slough off symptoms and tough out discomfort and pain while my usual tendency, so unlike my behavior that night, was to baby myself over every bellyache or bruise.

After I made the introductions, he and I thanked the women for getting me home. It was late. They declined the invitation to come inside, waved good-bye, and were off. Andy and I started up the flagstone path leading to the kitchen porch of our stone and shingle ranch. I felt pretty normal. My legs were working fine and everything around me looked as it should. I thought all I needed was a good meal to set everything right. I followed Andy into the house and straight to the dining room where he was in the middle of a late-night dinner. He had arrived home from aikido practice only a short while before. He brought me a plate and we sat down to eat together.

"So, what's going on?" he asked.

"It's nothing," I said. "I feel fine now. I just should have eaten dinner. My blood sugar must have dropped or something."

I told him I would call Dr. Marer, my primary, in the morning. But he kept questioning, wanting to know what exactly had happened. So I told him about the forays into Flatland and loss of movement and speech. Andy put down his fork and stared at me.

"I don't know," he said. "This doesn't sound like low blood sugar."

He was not a worrier. His mind didn't go racing off, trailing a litany of what-ifs as mine was wont to do. But he wasn't keen on my plan to wait until morning to contact the doctor.

"At least let's call Rich," he said. Richard was married to Andy's sister, Debbie. She was a nurse and he, a physician. I

My Father the Fish

offered a weak objection then gave in because despite my denial I was a little bit afraid. As Andy described my symptoms to Richard, his expression changed.

"Rich thinks you need to get to an emergency room right away," he said to me.

A trip to the hospital had not been on my to-do list. It was late and I was exhausted. Why spend god knows how many hours sitting in an ER waiting room only to be told to go home, eat something, and rest? I knew all too well from my experience with my dad what a trip to the ER meant. Nine years earlier, I had rushed him to the hospital in mid-afternoon. He was in excruciating, groaning, face-contorting pain. Yet we sat in the waiting room until late into the evening when his name was finally called. Then there were many more hours with him laid out on a gurney in the middle of a bustling emergency room. There was only one reason I had agreed to the call to Richard in the first place. I expected him to set our minds at ease and send me off to bed. I reached out my hand and Andy passed me the phone.

"Hi, Rich," I said. "Listen, this whole thing is getting blown out of all proportion. I'm fine now. Really. Whatever it was passed."

Richard, though, wasn't interested in whether the symptoms had passed or not. He said they could indicate a TIA—transient ischemic attack—the kind of mini-strokes my father had had, or spinal meningitis. I needed to be checked out as soon as possible. My heart took off like a sprinter as I considered Rich's words. What if there really was something wrong? Something serious. I was spooked by his short list of possible diagnoses and his ominous tone. As much as I was hell-bent on denying my symptoms were anything other than a passing anomaly, I was becoming alarmed. And there was more. For many years, I had harbored a belief I would fall victim to some horrible disease, probably cancer. There was no basis for this belief, no genetic predisposition or history of poor health, it was a gut feeling that something in my body was going to go very wrong.

Going to the ER terrified me. I mistrusted conventional medicine and had an almost pathological fear of hospitals. Over the years, I'd taken doctor-prescribed medications for one malady or another. The drugs often alleviated symptoms but failed to touch the underlying cause of the ailment, which would inevitably recur. Antibiotics left me with yeast infections and digestive problems that lasted months. Nasal sprays made my sinus congestion much worse—no one ever warned me about the rebound effect—and NSAIDS made me sick to my stomach. I was twenty-four when I was introduced to herbal medicine, acupuncture, and therapeutic massage. After a few weeks of herbal treatments I was forever relieved of a problem for which I had seen umpteen specialists and taken countless medications for more than eight years.

After that I had avoided medical doctors. When I was sick I consulted with an acupuncturist, an herbalist, or a homeopathic physician. Each of these practitioners viewed illness as a red flag, warning of a system in need of rebalancing and not as a call to battle. Because they treated me as a whole person and not as an assemblage of body parts, they earned my allegiance. I saved visits to traditional medical doctors for times when all else failed.

When my dad had a stroke, I had been witness to what a scary place hospitals could be. Several doctors were involved in his treatment. Each focused on his own specialty, and the communication between the doctors was poor. Time and again, the right hand didn't know what the left hand was doing. I questioned the orders for certain tests. Why were they needed? Because, I was told, they would provide more information. So I followed this thread and asked how the results might affect the treatment plan. They wouldn't, the doctor said, and as far as I was concerned, that was that. My dad was eighty-one. He was semiconscious. No one was going to put him through an invasive procedure just to generate data to fatten his file. "No way," I told the doctor. My confidence in my dad's care plummeted.

Still, even with all these memories flashing their warnings like lights circumscribing a minefield, I was afraid of dying, and I knew a TIA or meningitis was no small thing. So with reluctance I agreed to go to the ER. Andy called Dr. Marer to ask which of the two nearby hospitals we should go to, and she said she would notify Yale New Haven I was on the way. I went into the bedroom to change out of my slacks and heels and into sweatpants and sneakers. If I was going to sit for hours I might as well be comfortable. Andy, meanwhile, went to the basement to retrieve an overnight bag. He returned with a small red duffle, dropped it on the bed, and left me to finish getting ready.

The duffle unnerved me. Though I was usually one to prepare for all eventualities, being admitted to the hospital was not a possibility that had occurred to me. I unbuttoned and unzipped with the nonchalance of a woman changing out of her office clothes, ready to kick back after a long day at work. I picked up my slacks intending to hang them in the closet, but instead I carried them straight into a corner of the room and froze there. My face was only inches from the wall. Like a car stuck in neutral, I couldn't back up.

"Andy!" I screamed.

Some memories are readily accessible, others we protect ourselves from. In the moments before Andy raced into the room, there was a tapping inside the shell surrounding my guarded memories. A tap and then another tap, until one small image pecked its way through. The shell fell away, and other memories emerged:

I am standing stock-still in front of the refrigerator. I want the apple juice I know is inside, but my arms are refusing to heed the mind's command to open the door.

> *I am in my bedroom walking round and round in a tight circle, like yarn winding on a spindle. I can't stop.*
> *I am pouring coffee from a coffee pot. It splashes off the bananas and Heritage flakes that fill the cereal bowl resting on the counter next to my empty mug.*
> *I am sitting on the patio, warming in the sun. There is movement in the leaves. A chipmunk scampers inches from my feet, and a catbird wings its way across the yard. Only I am immobile, and I have slipped outside of time. I am at peace, dispassionate, observing the world like a scientist observes an experiment.*

The memories of these occurrences assembled themselves into a symptom picture extending at least six months into the past. I had not been okay for a long time. The occurrences had increased in frequency in the months prior to Flatland. I couldn't explain them, and for the most part I hadn't tried. I had dismissed some as spaciness or just plain inattention, and others were so short-lived I had run right past them in my race to get out the door to teach a class or go to the gym.

"What are you doing in the corner?" Andy asked, bursting into the room.

"I don't know," I whimpered. "I can't get out."

Andy walked over and with a hand on my shoulder turned me around. I collapsed against his chest. There was no more bravado. I was ready to go to the ER.

Two

Plastic chairs were arranged in rows of three throughout the waiting room of Yale New Haven Hospital. A young man in a varsity jacket hobbled on crutches. A wild-eyed lady talked to the air, and across the room a pregnant woman with a blank expression leaned into a man with an anxious face. Others sat staring or dozing off. The scene suggested late night in a bus station, but the idling ambulances, their flashing red lights bouncing off the plate glass window, were a constant reminder of where I was.

When we arrived, around 10:45 p.m., we headed for an official who stood at a podium as though she was the maitre'd. Dr. Marer had called ahead, and so we assumed we had a reservation. Wrong. Advance notice carried no weight. The woman added my name to her list and told us to take a seat. Andy kept glancing at the clock. After a half hour went by I wondered out loud if anyone ever up and died in the waiting room. Andy returned to the maitre'd to plead our case.

"Her doctor thinks she may be having a stroke," I heard him say. "Shouldn't she get in there right away?"

Could I really be having a stroke? I didn't think so, but as Andy continued to press the woman to get me in to see a doctor my anxiety escalated.

The woman either agreed with him or was not eager to accrue more unhappy customers. She ushered me ahead of the babbling drug addled, or maybe just crazy, lady and directed me to the ER receptionist to check in. I handed over my insurance card and answered a few questions about my symptoms. A nurse took my vitals and secured a name bracelet around my wrist. I eyed it with suspicion. Didn't she know I was a walk-in, who would soon be walking out?

We were told to retake our seats in the waiting room. It was another hour before my name was announced over the loud speaker, and we were led into a curtained cubicle. I perched on the edge of a gurney, and Andy sat down on a molded plastic chair. We waited some more. He scribbled in his pocket-sized notepad as he'd been doing ever since our arrival at the hospital. Later I would read his Dragnet-like account: 11:43 p.m. BP 117/73, pulse 91; 12:07 a.m. sodium chloride injection; 12:15 a.m. EKG, and so on, and so on. Andy was an environmental engineer. I thought this explained his passion for collecting and analyzing data, or perhaps it was the passion that explained his career choice. He calculated his gas mileage after every fill-up, noted the kilowatt-hours generated by our solar panels every day, and maintained records of first bloom dates of every flower, shrub, and tree on our property. That night he kept a detailed record of my medical ordeal. I thought the note taking may have given him a focus and helped him to stay calm, but it left me feeling less like his beloved and a little more like a lab experiment he was monitoring. Still, I couldn't begrudge him his coping mechanism if that was what it was. By this time, I was barely hanging on myself.

In short order I was visited by the triage nurse who asked me to recount the series of events that brought me to the ER. I became more agitated in the retelling and wondered when I would see a doctor. The nurse drew five vials of blood and left a port sticking in my arm. I was unsure of what its lingering presence might portend.

First year resident Dr. Adele Damlamian was the next to appear in the parade of nurses, med techs and doctors. She was petite with the face of a sixteen-year-old and a pleasant, professional manner that did much to offset the feeling a high school student was examining me. Her age and lack of experience aside, I was still relieved. Seeing a doctor made me feel safer. I was sure if I were stroking out she would know. Her lack of urgency in response to my reiteration of symptoms reassured me. Dr. Damlamian listened to my heart and lungs, scoped my eyes and throat, checked my reflexes and performed a neurological exam involving my touching my nose multiple times and following her hand movements. Before exiting my cubicle she ordered more tests—a CAT scan and an EKG—and told me she would be back once she had received the results.

Over the next several hours, periods of waiting were interrupted by visits from nurses in green scrubs and interns in white lab coats. Efficient technicians poked and prodded me. Each time a hand reached in to part the curtain, I recoiled turtle-like into my shell. Over and over I was asked, "What brought you here tonight?" Exasperated I laid out the litany of events again.

"Don't you guys talk to each other?" I blurted out at the next uniformed inquisitor.

The resident took a half step back, but quickly recovered. "Yes, of course we speak to each other. But you know, everyone picks up a little something different so it's helpful to hear you tell it and not have to rely on a second-hand report."

Ahhh, I thought, *that does make some sense, but still isn't there a better way?* Perhaps they could have all come in at once and circled round while I told my tale the first time? Did all of these questioners have a legitimate need to know? Having to keep repeating myself was exhausting and stressful. I wanted so badly to be taken care of, to feel I could rely on the doctors, but whatever wee bit of confidence I had to start with was being eroded.

I was getting claustrophobic cooped up in my cubicle when a man in scrubs arrived to take me for the CAT scan and EKG. I felt able to walk but he never gave me a chance. He wheeled my gurney down a long hallway. I don't remember if Andy came along, and I have no memory of the tests, or the trip back to the ER where a nurse in a printed

smock top and white pants handed me a small plastic cup.
"I need you to pee in this," she said.

I followed her down the hallway to the bathroom, glad to finally stretch my legs. I wasn't feeling dizzy, yet when I straddled the toilet I couldn't get a fix on where to put the cup. I kept adjusting it between my legs, moving it right then left, closer then further away. When I thought I finally had it in position, I let go… and urinated all over my hand. I hoped I had caught enough to satisfy the lab's requirements. I dried the cup with a paper towel and washed my hands. *What is wrong with me!* I thought. I was too embarrassed to tell the nurse what I'd done and was relieved when she pulled on a pair of latex gloves before taking the cup from me. When I told Andy what had happened, I cried. He assured me it was no big deal, nurses were used to that, but it was his arms wrapping around me, and not his words, that offered comfort.

A different nurse (how many were there?) administered a Breathalyzer test. She was apologetic but said they had to make sure my symptoms weren't due to intoxication. Was there any method to this madness? If drunkenness could explain my symptoms, why wasn't this checked first, before the blood draws and radiation? Once the machine confirmed that I was stone cold sober, I was left to try and relax while questioning the rationality of whomever it was that was calling the shots.

The cubicle was, if nothing else, my cubicle, a now-familiar space I shared with Andy. With the curtain drawn around us, I didn't have to see the sick and suffering waiting in hallways, the stainless steel carts full of medical implements, the nurses and interns padding through the halls from one crisis to another. I sat on my gurney, Andy sat on his chair by my side, and we tried to talk about ordinary things… what we would eat when we finally got out of there, plans for the weekend, and whether the laundry could wait a few days.

It was after 1 a.m. when Dr. Damlamian returned with results of the CAT scan. As she spoke, Andy took notes like mad, filling the pages of his notepad.

"A what on my brain?" I asked.

"A lesion," she said.

"What does that mean? Is it a wound of some kind?" I associated lesion with a bloody gash.

Dr. Damlamian explained that lesion was a general term for any abnormal or damaged tissue and could be due to any number of things like a viral infection or a trauma. An MRI would enable them to determine exactly what it was, but it appeared to be benign. *As in benign vs. malignant?* I thought. A slow paralysis crept over me. Dr. Damlamian had called it a 3 cm. lesion, not a tumor, and if she can't tell what it is without an MRI then how can she say it appears to be benign? She hurried out before I could get any further information.

Another three quarters of an hour passed before a neurologist appeared. He explained the episodes that had brought me to the ER were non-convulsive seizures of varying intensity and duration. He started me on medication to prevent further occurrences. Even after the report of a lesion and the explanation of the episodes, I was totally unprepared when he said he was admitting me for further evaluation. The sucker punch came as he turned to leave.

"You'll be seeing Dr. Bering," he said. "He's a neuro-oncologist."

I sat very still, breathless. Oncologist. A cancer doctor.

Alone again in the little cubicle, Andy took my hand. "Don't jump to any conclusions," he said. "They're only admitting you so they can do more tests. Get more information."

I couldn't even respond. I was jumping to all sorts of conclusions, none of them good. I wanted answers, right then. Not the next day, or the next.

At 4:30 a.m., almost six hours after we'd first arrived at the ER, a bed became available. Andy kept step alongside me as the transport attendant wheeled me through the hospital on the gurney.

"Almost there," said the attendant as he pushed me through a set of double doors. The sign above them read "Women's Oncology." That word again. I grabbed Andy's hand.

"This is all we've got for you now," said the attendant as he pushed me into a room. "As soon as a bed opens up in neurology we'll get you moved up there."

Relief rushed over me, like water breaking through a dam. *So, I don't belong here*, I thought, and soon drifted off to sleep, having no place else to hide.

A gentle hand was rousing me. *Andy?* No, not Andy. I had sent him home to get some sleep before he headed to his office. I didn't need him to hold my hand while I waited for test results. The ER doc had started me on meds that had curtailed the bouts of flatness, floating, and immobility. I felt fine, and I was still determined not to fold to the fear that smoldered at my heels like a bed of hot coals. It is just an emotion, I reasoned. I could stoke it or squelch it, here and now. Withhold the fuel, and the flame goes out.

The decisions we make, the directions we move in, are almost always the result of multiple force vectors nudging us this way or that. My decision to tell Andy to go home was no exception. It was true that I didn't want to succumb to childishness and cling to him in fear, but there was also another vector— a voice in my head, chattering in a stage whisper, daring to be heard. It reminded me that Andy was already in the hole with vacation days, having used more than his allotment over the Jewish holidays. Missing a day of work now would be time-off without pay. If the test results turned up something more insidious than a mere virus we would need every penny of his paycheck. This voice laden with dark possibility was the one I could not bear to acknowledge.

Andy hadn't protested when I shooed him away. My guess was that he was relieved. It was much later that he admitted to me he too had been working hard to convince himself I was okay, that I'd suffered some neurological glitch, or the CAT scan had been misinterpreted. "I was glad you were acting so together," he told me. "It was reassuring." And reassurance was what he wanted.

Again, the hand. So if not Andy's, whose was it? The question formed then dissolved, exhaustion trumping curiosity. The patting against my shoulder continued with greater determination. My eyelids slit open then clamped shut as a bright light assaulted my pupils.

"I'm so sorry. Go back to sleep," said the nurse as she switched off her flashlight.

This wake and blind ritual, a check on the functioning of my autonomic nervous system, would be repeated. At each rude awakening, I imagined the always apologetic nurse with the flashlight was an unwilling accomplice to an evil Dr. Frankenstein who lurked deep in the bowels of the hospital.

♦♦♦

My bed was gliding over linoleum. It was 7:30 a.m., and a transport attendant was taking me for an EEG to be followed by an MRI. The neurologist who saw me in the ER had explained that the EEG mapped the electrical activity of the brain and would be used to diagnose the cause of my brain dysfunction. An array of wires extended from the machine. Each terminated in a plastic disc that the technician affixed to my scalp with sticky goo. There was no mirror in the room and this was a good thing. Even without it my imagination ran wild conjuring images of strapped-down patients, electroshock therapy, and mad scientists. I was relieved when the test was completed.

Once again, I was on the move. The transport attendant rolled me through the hallways of the hospital, into and out of an elevator and then down more hallways. I remembered when it had been my father on the gurney and me keeping pace by his side. I had been his companion and advocate. Unable to speak, shrunken and frail, he hadn't the ability to protest or get up off the gurney. As I recalled how powerless he had been, I shuddered, and though in the here and now, I was capable of standing up and walking away, I nonetheless felt vulnerable and at the mercy of the hospital with all its moving parts, one relentless gear engaging with the next.

The radiology technician in charge of the MRI positioned me on my back on a narrow platform that would ferry me into the hollow core of the magnet. My head was immobilized between padded clamps, earplugs protected my ears and a cotton blanket was tucked around me.

"It will take about forty-five minutes to complete the scan of your brain," the tech informed me. "You will have to lie perfectly still the whole time."

"What if something goes wrong with me while I'm in there? What if I have another seizure?" I asked, swallowing hard to push back the panic.

"No problem," said the technician placing a call button in my hand. "Press this, and I'll know you need help."

Easier said than done, I thought, remembering the difficulty I had the previous evening trying to unlock the car door. *I could die in here without ever seeing Andy again! He will be devastated.* I could not imagine what my own death would be like for me. There was no reliable model for this, but having lost my best friend, my spiritual teacher, and my father, I knew all about grief. I could picture Andy chanting *kaddish*: swaying back and forth, *tallis* drawn over his head, tears staining the pages of the *siddur*. My mother would sit, immobile and numb, eyes reddened but face a blank. Matt, my brother, would be running, directing, frantic to keep the sorrow at bay. As painful as it was to conjure up these scenes it was preferable to facing the terror I felt each time I thought the words, *I could die in here.*

Like a conveyor belt at a canning plant, the platform carried me head first into the belly of the machine. Confined and unable to move, I felt like a sardine packed tight in a tin. The noise from the machine was deafening despite the ear protection—a thunderous rat-a-tat-tat like a jackhammer pounding concrete. Yet, I fell asleep only to be awakened by the jarring silence at the conclusion of the scan.

It was late that same morning when the radiology technician wheeled me into the hall. It was wide and spare—unadorned white walls, linoleum flooring, fluorescent lights. All the doors were closed.

"Warm enough?" The tech asked.

I nodded.

"Someone will come get you soon." And with that, he left me laying there on the gurney like a parcel awaiting pickup.

Where is this hospital, anyway? I realized I didn't know. We had arrived at night, and I'd never been there before. I wasn't sure which street it was on, or how I could get home from there in my stocking feet with no coat, phone, or wallet. My heart thrummed in my ears, my chest hollow, empty as the hallway. I felt alone and forsaken, and my blame fell not on anyone in particular, but on the machinery of the hospital itself. It was a high tech mill, and I was nothing more than a sack of grist.

Soon, an attendant did arrive and wheeled me to my new room in the neurology wing. I was relieved to be out of the oncology ward. The new room was pretty much the same as my last one. There was a small closet, a night table with a couple of drawers and a rolling tray table that reached across the bed. The room was equipped for two, but the other bed was unoccupied. That was a relief. I didn't want to be compelled to chitchat, or worse, listen to another's moans.

Before taking his leave, the attendant pulled a large white plastic bag and my small red duffle off the shelf mounted underneath the bed. The plastic bag contained my hat, scarf, coat, and shoes. The duffle held the things I had tossed inside before we left for the ER: a well-worn copy of *Transcendental Aim*, my journal, a few toiletries, and clean socks and underwear.

I was tired from the night of little sleep, but otherwise felt fine. I busied myself putting my few belongings away. The simple act of choosing where to rest my book, place my shoes, and hang my jacket restored a small measure of lost autonomy. The presence of my toothbrush, journal, and book were proof this was *my* room. I may not have known where in New Haven the hospital was located, but I knew I had a room of my own there, and that was comforting. My few belongings in place, I climbed into bed with renewed self-confidence and fell asleep.

When I awoke a short time later, I was tethered to a pole by plastic tubing running from an IV catheter in my arm, and my stomach was rumbling. In the ER the night before, I had been told I couldn't eat until my evaluation was complete. *Is it?* I wondered. *Can I eat now? Am I allowed to leave my room?* It was 11:00 a.m., and I was starving. I waited for someone to come check on me. Like a token on a game board, I had been advanced one square or more, but I still had no idea who the Player was or the rules of the game. I carefully slid off the bed, took hold of the IV pole and rolled it alongside me as I tiptoed to the door and peered down the deserted hallway. Grumbles and growls (the complaints from my stomach) disturbed the quiet. I headed out the door. A left turn at the end of the hall brought me to a nurse's station. There, I identified myself as the new patient in room 224 and asked if I was allowed to have anything to eat. The nurse looked up at me with an expression that I read as equal parts shock and chagrin.

"You haven't eaten?" She asked. "Didn't you order breakfast?"

"No. I didn't order anything," I said. "Won't someone just bring me a tray?"

Apparently not. Things had changed since my last hospital stay when I was eight. It had been a brief one, the result of a car accident. The nurse sent me back to my room, and in a short while a candy striper arrived to show me the ropes of hospital life beginning with Basic Sustenance 101. She handed me an extensive menu of breakfast, lunch, and dinner items. I was thrilled to find Mexican beans and rice, alfalfa sprouts, and soymilk on the menu. *Very trendy*, I thought. *And just right for my palate.*

After I'd ordered, I lay down again hoping to get some rest while I waited for my meal to arrive. But I couldn't settle down. I ruminated, my questions piling one on top of another. *What's wrong with me? What caused the brain lesion? Is it a wound, like a cut that will heal? Is it a virus, that will get better on its own? What about the MRI, what did it show? And who's my doctor? Who's calling the shots?* It surely was not me.

So many questions and no sign of answers. The waiting was intolerable; the not knowing, unbearable. Small armies marched in my belly. I was jubilant when my lunch tray was finally placed in front of me, and I ate the simple meal with relish. After I'd cleaned my plate, I picked up my journal and pen, wrote down the date, and stared at the blank page. My thoughts were dark and I was reluctant to commit them to paper.

At the sound of footsteps, I looked up. A nurse stood at the foot of my bed. She was armed with a hypodermic.

"What's that?" I asked.

Heparin, she told me. A blood thinner.

"Why do I need it?"

With a sweet smile and a chipper tone, she explained that lying in bed for extended periods of time increases the risk of a blood clot.

"I see," I said. "Well, how about I simply get up and move around?"

It wasn't up to her, she said. The doctor had ordered the medication. It was written in my chart, which apparently made it sacrosanct.

An alarm sounded. Rubber-soled shoes skittered down the hallway. A janitor wheeled his cart by my door, trailing a hint of disinfectant.

"I don't want it," I said.

"It's routine," she said. "Just a preventative."

I stared at her. *Does she think being routine makes it reasonable? Where's the logic in that? Don't I factor into the equation of care at all?*

"I don't need heparin. I am not confined to bed," I said.

"It's doctor's orders," she protested.

"Well, tell the doctor I refused it. If he has a problem with that he can come speak to me."

At least then, I thought, *I'd get to meet the man or woman behind the curtain.* I was more than a little bit frustrated. Someone was ordering all the tests and drugs, but I had yet to meet my doctor.

She slowly retracted and lowered the hypodermic as though holstering a sidearm. Emboldened by her retreat, I continued.

"What's in this IV?" I asked, pointing to the drip bag.

Saline solution, needed to keep me hydrated, the nurse reported.

"Please unhook me," I said. "I'm not at risk of dehydrating."

She followed my gaze to the empty soup bowl, drained coffee cup, and half empty pitcher of water sitting on my lunch tray.

"Okay," she said without a fight, and unplugging the plastic tubing she set me free.

What a relief! I sprang off the bed and pushed it over to the wall, leaving an open space in the center of the room. I planted my feet, drew my shoulders back and down, tucked my chin, and lowered my chest. Exhaling as I relaxed my belly and dropped my weight into my legs, I rotated my forearms and floated them upward. Focusing on the slow even rhythm of this tai chi chuan form brought temporary respite from anxiety and boredom. I still had no idea what was in store for me.

Later, I reached for *Transcendental Aim*. The cover, once textured and sky blue, was faded and worn smooth. The pages were loose in their binding. I'd read the slim volume countless times. It contained a collection of talks given by Dr. Robert C. Sohn, the man I call Gurudev, a Sanskrit word meaning a spiritual master—one who dispels darkness and points the way to light. The talks were originally spoken to a small group of twenty-five disciples, of whom I was one.

I met Gurudev in 1977. I was twenty-three years old, and I had been looking for an answer to the question, *What's the point?*, ever since my best friend, Marcia, was killed by a drunk driver while we were both in high school. Her death had hit me with the seismic force of an earthquake, crumbling the foundation on which I had stood for all my sixteen years. I knew some people die young but knowing in the abstract was different than knowing from experience. It was Marcia's death in particular I couldn't make sense of. She had everything to live for. Finally, she'd be breaking out of high school, heading to college, a boyfriend, and freedom. Marcia and I talked all the time about losing our virginity. If either of us had had a bucket list *have sex* would have been number one. How could she have died when she hadn't even become a woman?

If one's life could end before it ever really got started, before one did any of the really important things, then what was the point? This was no small question for me. I asked anyone and everyone for their take on why we were here. I didn't get a single satisfactory answer. I got very few answers at all, and knowing the truth was imperative. Once the

27

question occurred to me, I could hardly believe I'd never thought to ask it before. How could one go on without knowing the point? For this world to exist in all its complexity without purpose was inconceivable to me. How could human beings be born only to die? There had to be something I wasn't seeing. A reason for being. I was desperate to understand both *the point* and the role I was meant to play in relationship to it. I longed for a purpose and was desperate for direction.

In the seven years that followed Marcia's death, I looked for answers in the tangle of my own Jewish roots. I combed the sacred yogic texts of the East, read the Chinese philosophers, and explored the occult, but nowhere did I find an answer that rang true for me. Then, a series of events I had in no way orchestrated landed me at the feet of Dr. Robert C. Sohn. He had answers that held up when tested against the barometer of my own life experience. Over the next couple of years, he had me looking at the world through new eyes. "If you look at the world in a new way," he wrote in *Tao and T'ai Chi Kung*, "you will see a new world, and you will be a new part of that new world." In time, that was my experience, exactly. I transformed.

Gurudev became my spiritual teacher, always pointing the way back to God—which, it turned out, is *the point*. There are many paths that lead to God, and I had stumbled over several of them during my years-long search. The problem was, I hadn't understood what I was reading or hearing. I had come into contact with fragments of a teaching, never the whole. Gurudev expressed the underlying cosmology and the principles of spiritual work in a language I could understand. He taught that at root, in our essence, we are not, any one of us, other than God. He called that essential root, the Self. The Self, is not the body, not thought or emotion. The Self doesn't act, it witnesses. It is none other than God's reflection in the world as we know it. Gurudev always referred to the Self with a capital "S" to distinguish it from the many little selves that make up the multi-faceted personality. I came to think of those selves, each with their own preferences, aversions, motivations and patterns of behavior, as the cast of characters in a play. In my case, each cast member responded to the name Lorri and referred to itself with the same singular pronoun: I or me. The Self, on the other hand, is One, indivisible, unchanging, eternal.

The cast answering to the name Lorri is energy in motion, a constant state of flux. In one moment, Lorri can be as charitable as Mother Teresa, in another, vindictive and miserly as a Scrooge; Monday morning a confident leader and by afternoon a sniveling child. Since the descriptors most often used to define God are terms like ineffable, infinite, omnipresent, eternal, and unconditionally loving—in other words, terms that defy the imagination—recognizing God within is challenging. One of the traditional methods for meeting this challenge is self-observation—taking a careful and uncritical look at oneself again and again and again, and asking, is what I see God? That bitch in me, is she unconditionally loving? The terrified child that made a brief appearance in Lorri's name—eternal, omnipresent? *I don't think so.* This process of separating the Self from the many little selves in order to realize God within, is what Gurudev called spiritual work or simply, "The Work". Bit by bit, strip away the many selves, and beneath this husk of personality God can be found.

Even after he died in 1997, Gurudev's teachings remained at the hub of the wheel around which my life turned. No one that knew me well would have been surprised that *Transcendental Aim* was the one book I had thrown in my duffle the night before. I was afraid. I needed strength, and what could be more fortifying than a reminder of my inherent godliness and life's impermanence?

I opened the book at random and began to read but didn't absorb the words. They were obliterated by the anxious stream of questions running through my head. If I had taken in the text, I would have remembered my aim to know God within. I would have encountered the truth that the body is a fleeting reality. It will die and Lorri will die with it. Those words alone would have altered my perspective, rendering inconsequential my feelings, my thoughts and my experiences of Flatland, trips to the ER and lesions on the brain.

Frustrated, I dropped the book and picked up a newspaper I had found abandoned on a chair in the hallway. I poked at the crossword puzzle for a bit and then made a list of things I might need if I couldn't go home that night. There was a shift change and a new nurse arrived with heparin. I had an easier time warding her off. I asked if she knew when I'd be seeing a doctor. She didn't. While I waited I considered two possible outcomes: I know this is all going to turn out to be nothing, a freak event, a chemical imbalance; or, no matter how bad it is, cancer even, I will survive it.

This day might be my last, or it might not, I thought. *Either way, it doesn't change what I have to do now.*

My head was full of principles and practices and teaching tales that had taken root there. Gurudev had left me with all I needed to pull myself up, over, and out of the throes of this latest turmoil. But, as the hours passed, my thoughts continued to go round and round like a horse on a carousel. I kept reaching for the brass ring that could be redeemed for a higher, more encompassing perspective from which to view my situation or, at the very least, a state of calm from which I could think clearly. Gurudev had often told the story of the Indian *mahout*.

Once upon a time there was a wise old mahout in charge of the care and training of three great elephants. When one of the elephants became unruly, stomping and trumpeting, the mahout coaxed his other two elephants to stand on either side of the belligerent beast. Their presence there, gently pressing up against the sides of the troublesome pachyderm, brought it under control.

Unpacking the metaphor, Gurudev had explained the unruly elephant represented a man's emotions. The other two represented, respectively, a man's mind and body. Only when the mind and body worked together toward the same end could the emotions be subdued and equanimity restored. *What were my elephants up to?* I thought. My emotions were overwrought, that was apparent. Where were mind and body and how could they be brought into play? I laid against the pillows, closed my eyes and scanned my body from head to toe, noted where I felt tension in my muscles and breathed into each knot until it released some. Using my mind, I observed the fearful imaginings projected on the screen inside my head and the passing parade of what ifs. I moved my attention to what I knew to be true. I have a body, but I am not the body, nor my thoughts, nor the knot-tying emotions. I am the Self, God within, eternal, unchanging. Within moments, I was infused with a steadying calm. For the time being, the troublesome elephant had been brought into line. Centered and grounded, I reached for the floor with my feet and set off down the corridor.

There are many people here who are worse off than me, I thought. *They may be lonely and scared and feeling as helpless and objectified as I do.* I looked into one room after another.

"Good afternoon" I said.

"Oh. Good afternoon," chirped a bald woman.

Chemo? I guessed, with a wordless smile back in her direction.

In the next room a woman sat watching television. A multitude of electrodes, like tentacles of different colors, connected her head to a motherboard mounted behind the bed. I wondered what was wrong with her and whether I had the same problem. She raised her eyes from her laptop, smiled and gave a slight nod. This I found reassuring.

Other patients were asleep or returned my greeting with blank stares, but I persisted making my way from room to room with increasing ease. Passing by a visitors' lounge, I spied a computer available for public use. I stopped to check my email in case there were messages from a client that required response. Though I was in the process of making a career shift, I still did regulatory work in the dietary supplement industry, advising clients on labeling and compliance issues. In retrospect, this checking of email, a feature of my ordinary life, was an absurd thing to be doing given the circumstances, but I was clinging to the hope I'd be sent home by the end of the day, with a diagnosis of infection and a prescription for a cure.

Back in my room, I considered calling Andy, but what would I say? There was no news. Why bother him? He was probably eating lunch about now. Andy and his lunch. Always the same. One and a half peanut butter and jelly sandwiches on whole grain bread, organic Valencia peanuts preferred. A baggie of carrot or celery sticks, a 6-ounce jar of homemade yogurt topped with two pitted prunes cut into quarters, and for dessert, a piece of fruit. Today it would be an apple, I thought, remembering what was left in the fridge.

I knew Andy ate at his desk where he could study without questioning stares or interruptions. Between bites, he read the weekly Torah portion, looking up the words he didn't know in a Hebrew-English dictionary of Talmudic literature. He wrote the definitions on blank pages in his weekly planner, using a mechanical pencil. His lettering was so small I often could not discern it, his Hebrew script somewhat easier to read than his English. I smiled. It was no wonder he had no pals at work. His coworkers must think him quite an odd duck, but I admired his discipline.

Discipline was a practice I knew something about. Once Gurudev accepted me as his disciple, I moved into the Gatsby era mansion he shared with Tina, his wife—whom we called Mataji—their two children, and his twenty-five closest students. The forty-room Georgian style colossus situated on the Gold Coast of Long Island was home to our spiritual community, an ashram. Our life was a disciplined one, framed by daily practices and useful work that maintained and contributed to our household.

We rose at six each morning and gathered in the room we called the temple to meditate, chant, practice tai chi, and listen to Gurudev discourse on Samkhya yoga philosophy and the esoteric psychology and cosmological teaching of G.I. Gurdjieff. Over the years, we engaged in other practices and studies as well, including *nada* yoga (the yoga of sound), *pranayama* (breathing exercises), *amma* (Mataji's own system of therapeutic massage), logic, and quantum physics. Temple was where Gurudev addressed specific difficulties one or another of us was having with our spiritual practice.

At 10 a.m., we gathered for brunch and then set off to attend to the day's work. We earned our livelihood at The Wholistic Health Center and Institute for Self-Development—a clinic and school founded by Gurudev and Mataji, in nearby Manhasset. Some of us were health professionals, some teachers, and others, including myself, saw to the running of the businesses. We all participated in maintaining a spotless home, nurturing an organic garden, and manicuring fourteen acres of lawn, flowering shrubs, and stately trees.

In the evening, we gathered to practice tai chi before we each retired to our own bedroom, notebook in hand, to reflect upon the day and write up our observations and analysis of our own multifaceted personality at work and play. For me, this was the toughest part of the day. I was tired, and this period of reflection required a self-honesty that was often painful. My analysis began with a detailed accounting of the patterns of thought, feeling, and behavior I had observed in myself that day. Then, I would document the efforts I had made to act against them and finally evaluate the patterns from the perspective of a spiritual aim.

The questions I had to ask myself over and over were

"Are my patterns of thought, emotion, and action moving me closer to knowing God, or pushing me further away? In any given moment, am I aware of the unchanging Self, or have I mistakenly assumed that a single part of my chameleon-like personality is who I really am? By midnight I would add my notebook to the growing pile at Gurudev's bedroom door. He would collect them and before the end of the next day we would find them once again stacked in a pile at his door, newly annotated with helpful comments on our analysis and efforts in light of a spiritual aim. He called this practice driver analysis, because the aspects of personality under observation could and did drive the action every which way. I wrote a driver analysis virtually every night for twenty years.

The self-discipline I developed during my ten years in the ashram enabled me to bear discomfort with some degree of neutrality, to overcome much laziness, and to exercise patience. It also made it possible for me to attain a level of excellence in many facets of my life that would not have been otherwise possible. As much as the daily subjugation of my personal preferences was often frustrating and infuriating, I have never regretted my decision to put myself under Gurudev's direction. After wandering for years asking What's the point?, I had finally come upon a man who knew the answer. When he said, "Come follow me," I did the only intelligent thing. I followed.

My parents thought I was crazy—brainwashed, actually. They could not understand how I could allow someone else to determine to such a degree how I was living my daily life. Even more incomprehensible to them was the fact that in the ashram, we lived as a collective. All income generated went into one communal pot. I hadn't a cent to my name, and this along with my lack of health insurance affronted their middle-class sensibilities. But more than that, they were terrified for me. They were sure I had fallen under the influence of another Jim Jones.

My Father the Fish

My move into the ashram had taken place almost exactly a year after the mass suicide at Jonestown, and every spiritual or quasi-spiritual group was being scrutinized in the press for cultish overtones, brainwashing, and corruption of the young. It's no wonder my parents were out of their minds with worry, and it was many years before they were ready to admit I had not been brainwashed or victimized, but rather had flourished and grown in innumerable ways during my time with Gurudev. It was also many years before I had compassion for them, before I appreciated how much they loved me and had been, like any normal parents, hell-bent on protecting their young.

Bottles rattled, an orderly pushed a cart past my open door, and my mind snapped to the here and now. Hospital. Waiting. I again picked up my book, but the question Andy had asked on the way to the ER vied for my attention like a four-year-old skipping up and down, arms waving. Why hadn't I pulled off the road? This was a question I would come to hear again and again from others, too. My answer was always the same: "I just didn't think of it. I never thought what was happening was serious. I figured it would pass." There was a glimmer of truth in all that, but my gut told me there was something more, loitering a hair beyond my grasp, calling out to me in a barely audible whisper. I sensed it was a pivotal point on which my life would turn, so I listened harder.

Why would I continue driving, risking my life and the lives of others just to get to a meeting? *That's obvious*, I thought. *This wasn't just any meeting.* It was the opportunity I had been waiting for to network with the very people who had the clout to help me jump-start the new career I was ready to launch. I had spent many years in the business world. For quite sometime I had wanted to make a change, to do work that would benefit people in some real and meaningful way. In 2002, six years before I drove my car through Flatland, I had set in motion a plan that was only now ready to bear fruit. It was in that year I met Reb Zalman Schachter-Shalomi. He was a rabbi and a *chassid*, but of greater significance to me, he was a *rebbe*.

"A rabbi hears what you say with your mouth," wrote Rabbi Aron Moss, "a rebbe hears what you are saying with your soul." Five years after the death of Gurudev, I was very much in need of a soul whisperer.

When Gurudev departed this earth, he left his words—in writings and recordings—but not the dynamism and energy of his living presence. I missed his good humor, his encouragement, and even his kicks in the butt. Gurudev had been like a shepherd tending his sheep, prodding with gentle nudges and sometimes shoves and shouts, but always heading his flock in the direction of home. As the life I had lived with Gurudev slipped further into the past, I felt more and more like a lost sheep. I desperately needed to re-anchor myself in The Work, to repair the fraying rope. This new career was the hemp from which I would wind those stronger strands. It had been a long time coming and I was frantic to begin.

Also, I had made a promise to myself to repay Gurudev for all he had done for me. Of course, repayment was an odd concept to be considering since he was already dead, but more than that, it countered an aphorism he himself had often quoted: "God, your parents, and your teachers can never be repaid." It was a debt too enormous to fathom. *Still, it wouldn't hurt to try.*

If I could find work that would allow me to share his teaching with others, it would be a step in the right direction, at the very least an expression of gratitude. And I wanted to make Gurudev proud, to show him all the time and energy he had put into guiding and cultivating my spiritual development had borne fruit. I believed without a doubt that on whatever celestial plane his soul now rested, we were still connected, and he would know what I was doing and why.

"My job feels empty to me. No meaning, no purpose." I told Reb Zalman that June day as we sat together around a picnic table at *Elat Chayiim*, a Jewish retreat center in the Catskills. He sat stroking his long white beard, as I described my relationship with Gurudev and explained how it had fueled my growth.

"I have a lot to give, but I don't know where to give it." I said. "I'm ready to leave my job, to do something entirely different. But what? I have no idea."

Reb Zalman asked me a few questions about myself and about what I had been doing over the last few years since Gurudev died. I described my consulting work and the volunteering I had done in Israel. Every Shabbat, I had taken a group of elderly women from their assisted living residence for a walk through their neighborhood. It helped them to reconnect to a life they felt they had lost, and making it possible for them to do so was satisfying to me. Hearing this, he suggested I read his book *From Aging to Sage-ing: A Profound New Vision of Growing Older*.

"Perhaps," he had said, "there you will find a direction for your work to take."

In the book, Reb Zalman identified the second half of life as the time for taking on the tasks of life completion and embracing what he called sage-ing˙: the process of looking inward to harvest the wisdom gleaned from years of experience. A lengthy appendix to the book provided contemplative tools and exercises for deep inner exploration: a how-to manual of sorts. Later, reading the book, I was intrigued by the concepts laid forth. The focus on self-examination and development of a spiritual life was in line with the values and practices that guided my life. *This*, I thought, *was something I could do well. This was something I could*

˙ ® sage-ing is a registered trademark of Sage-ing International

37

teach.

    I set out to earn certification in the sage-ing work, but the planets were not aligned. The institute that taught the program had folded and it would be some years before a newly formed Sage-ing Guild offered the teacher training program. During that time I turned fifty, cut my consulting work by half, and earned a Master of Science in Jewish Studies focused on aging, death, and dying. The focus combined my interest in the experience of elderhood with my desire to learn more about Jewish practices and principles.

    I grew up as a bagels-and-lox-Jew. I knew what to eat on which holiday but had no idea what Jews believed in. Andy, on the other hand, had a solid Jewish education and he was observant. He prayed three times every day, followed kosher dietary laws, and observed the Sabbath as a day of refraining from work, phone, car, internet, TV and more. When we first met, I thought we were headed in the same direction albeit via different paths, but I was no longer sure that was true. I didn't understand the aim of his practices, and he wasn't very good at providing answers to my questions. I thought if I learned firsthand what was behind the things he did we could communicate better about the ideas that were important to me.

    That explained why I pursued Jewish Studies. Why I set out to earn a master's at all was a different matter. When I first met Gurudev I had been headed for grad school, but then as my life took a different direction those plans fell by the wayside, and I no longer saw a need for an advanced degree. Yet most everyone I knew had a trail of letters after their name, and deep down I always regretted that I didn't. I felt inadequate.

    By the time I completed the degree and the training that allowed me to add an MS and a CSL (Certified Sage-ing Leader) after my name, it was 2008, a couple of months before my drive through Flatland. I had done market research, designed a business card and brochure, and put together a PowerPoint presentation. I had scheduled meetings with directors of senior centers. My calendar was filled. I was finally ready to head down a new professional path—and that had its own appeal. When I failed to remember the truth of God within, self-doubt and self-hate overtook me. Then, only the good opinion of others mattered. I relished an opportunity to succeed. If the people I touched saw merit in me, than when I looked in the mirror perhaps I would see that, too.

First on my launch agenda was the meeting at the Hamden Library. Representatives of the Area Office on Aging would be there. I had imagined myself greeting these new colleagues and describing my program offerings in a witty and engaging manner. My audience would be approving, both intrigued with the subject matter and receptive to my approach to helping seniors grow emotionally, intellectually, and spiritually. I was ready to rock and roll. I was fired up with aim and purpose. This meeting was a stepping-stone to a career that had been a long time in coming, a career I was counting on to fortify my connection to the Work. That connection was my lifeline. Losing it would be losing the only thing that really mattered. Of course I had to continue on to the meeting. *Wouldn't anyone have?*

Three

Later on, that first full day in the hospital, a clean-shaven man in a white lab coat stepped into my room, nodded at the nurse fiddling with a monitor, and introduced himself. I eyed him with caution. Like the female resident I had seen in the ER, he looked too young to be a doctor. Dangling over the side of the bed, my fidgety legs drew his attention to wooly-socked feet. I wished I were behind a desk wearing a smart skirt and heels. If there was an imbalance of power in that small room I was sure the deficit lay on my side of the scales.

Dr. Gardiner got right down to business. Upbeat and direct, a news anchor reporting on a breaking story. "I've seen the MRI. You have a brain tumor—one of two possible types: a glioblastoma multiforme or a meningioma."

As he droned on, I watched his mouth move, but like a bird in a bramble my ears were caught on the words *brain tumor*.

How is this possible? I'm healthy. There must be some mistake, I thought. Had they even checked my blood sugar? My hormone levels? I scrambled, grasping for an alternative diagnosis. The ER doctor had said the CAT scan showed a lesion that could be caused by several things, one of which was a virus. This was the possibility I had been banking on. A virus. How bad could that be—a cold was a virus, right? I grabbed a pen and scrap of paper ready now to scribble down his every word.

"Those things you said, glio and meningee something, are they cancer?" I asked.

"Yes they are, but only the glioblastoma is highly aggressive," he said. His words were a tidbit, dropped into my mouth like a mama bird depositing a morsel of agreeable news. Still, I felt whacked but good and reeled from the word cancer. The big C.

The nurse stopped her fiddling and stepped in closer to me. I was down for the count, but Dr. Gardiner seemed not to notice. He continued on in doctor-speak. I caught only half sentences, occasional words, as he looped his way from necrosis to edema to parietal lobes.

"So the tumor could be either type," I said. "What are the chances?"

"Oh, I'd say 50-50. It resembles a meningioma but the MRI, as I said, shows necrosis and a hollow which is a feature typical of the glioblastoma."

In other words, I thought, *either I've got a bad brain tumor or a VERY bad brain tumor.* His words confounded my wounded ears and accelerated my retreat into confusion. I would later learn meningiomas are very slow growing and are, for all intents and purposes, treated as though they were benign—still a brain tumor—but no need to run out and buy a cemetery plot.

"So what happens now?"

"A biopsy. To determine exactly what we have here."

My eyes widened. "But the tumor is in my brain. How can you biopsy my brain?"

Dr. Gardiner paused as though considering my question. "With surgery," he said.

A montage of scenes from horror films flashed before my mind's eye: chainsaws, axes, bloody heads, and jagged scars. *They want to saw my head open and cut out a piece of my brain!*

"When?" I asked Dr. Gardiner.

"Not before tomorrow," he said, as though tomorrow resided somewhere in the distant future. Then, having wrapped up his newscast, Dr. Gardiner turned to leave.

"Oh, one more thing," he said, pausing at the door. "The neurosurgical team will review your MRI in the morning and discuss a treatment plan with you."

Okay, I breathed. A plan. That sounded good. I liked plans.

As my eyes followed him out the door, a delicate but firm hand reached for mine. The nurse, who had heard all, asked if I would like her to call the chaplain.

It took a moment for her question to register and when it did it was with the impact of an H-bomb. *Oh god*, I thought. *She thinks I'm going to die.* As far as I was concerned, the offer of a chaplain, coming from a nurse who actually understood the diagnosis, carried the weight of a confirming second opinion. No, I emphatically did not want to see a chaplain. Not yet, anyway. I wanted to be alone, and I needed to call Andy at work. It killed me to have to tell him this, but what could I do? He picked up after the first ring.

"A doctor finally came," I said. "He saw the MRI. It's not good. He said I've got..." I couldn't finish the sentence. The words *brain tumor* tumbled back at me. Beating out those three syllables on his tender eardrums, piercing his adoring heart, it was more than I could shoulder.

"Lorri, got what? Are you there?"

"Yes, I'm here," I said. "I've got a brain tumor." Had he seen my face, it would have appeared a stony mask—the finishing touch on a full-body fortification erected to keep the news at a distance and hysteria at bay.

Andy listened without interrupting as I repeated Dr. Gardiner's report. When he responded it was with a measured calm—none of his usual optimistic bounce.

"He didn't give you a definitive diagnosis," he said. "We need more information. So let's not get ahead of ourselves. Slow down. We'll take one step at a time."

"Right." I said. "Nothing definitive. Could be either type."

Then there was silence. Seconds? Minutes? It felt endless, then...

"Babes, you are strong and, except for this, in really good health. That's a big plus. It will go a long way toward a positive outcome."

Andy may have taken a knock-out blow, but now he was back in the ring, upbeat as usual. It was just like Andy, and very unlike me to look for the positive. I tended to see only half-empty cups. My nature was to run towards calamity like a river raft racing toward the falls. Andy always saw the promise of a rainbow after the storm. This was, perhaps, his nature, but then there was also the God factor.

Andy believed in a Grand Designer with a Grand Design. He had faith that every outcome was for the good and that God not only watched over him but also listened to his prayers. He prayed three times every day: prayers of praise, thanks, and request. As for myself, I hadn't seen much point to prayer. Did God need us to say, "God is great"? I could understand, "Thanks". Gratitude was a good thing for sure, but the prayers of beseeching? In my book these were absurd. The God I believed in was omniscient, omnipotent, and aloof. My God did not listen to prayers or otherwise meddle in people's lives. Still, though I had often challenged Andy on his beliefs, that day I was grateful at least one of us believed in a god who might listen. I needed to lean on Andy. If he got his support from leaning on God, well, that was fine with me. During our brief conversation, Andy was a rock. I never would have suspected that after we said good-bye, he left his desk, shut himself in a conference room, and wailed. But he did.

That morning, when I had sent Andy off to work, I was still counting on being sent home by the end of day with a scrawled prescription and assurances that all would be fine. A different scenario was unfolding now, and I wanted to scream and cry and crawl into his arms. But even so, I didn't tell him I needed him with me. I coolly suggested he finish out the workday, stop at the house and pick up a few things I might need, and then come to the hospital. Maybe he even offered to come right away, but if he did I'm sure I told him it wasn't necessary. Yet, as the hours passed, my disappointment in him and pity for myself mushroomed. Alone with the memory of Dr. Gardiner's words, all I knew was Andy should have come. Right away. No matter what I had said. I needed him. Why hadn't he known that?

It had always been hard for me to ask for what I needed, but blaming him for not reading my mind, or for not being my knight in shining armor on a galloping steed who would bound through the doorway to rescue me, was my problem, not his, and it was a setup for suffering. I hung up the phone and sank into the bed pillow, numb with terror and wishing for sleep. I was drifting off when a thought propelled me upright: *How would I tell my mother?* My father had died in 2007, and she was just beginning to resurface after two years submerged in grief. Could she handle this, or would she go to pieces again? And what if I died? Could my little brother, Matt, take care of her without my help? He was 100% there when she needed anything done from changing light bulbs to managing her investments, but when it came to the emotional stuff, Matt always looked to me to step in. My mother got easily overwhelmed and then didn't function well. How could I tell her over the phone? Concerning myself with my mother allowed me to sidestep the panic that came with contemplating the possibility of my own imminent death. When my mind drifted in that direction, it was nothing but a free fall, jumping without a parachute. Faith in my philosophy of life and its ultimate purpose, which included death, flew right out the window.

I called Matt, told him I was in the hospital, and brought him up to date. He was stunned. He said little. What could he say? Then I brought up Mom, and we plotted. He came up with a strategy. He was good at that, just like I was. We were both high functioning and efficient. He was also hands on, like our dad had been—a real mister fix-it around the house. Matt looked like Dad too—barrel chested, narrow hipped and balding. Now, he took charge, as our dad would have done. He said he would call Mom and tell her he was in her neighborhood seeing a client and would like to take her out to dinner afterwards. We both knew she would love that and not be suspicious. That way, when I called to tell her about the brain tumor I could be sure she wasn't alone.

Matt assured me he would drive Mom up to Connecticut in the morning so they could be there for the biopsy whenever that would be. I made a few tweaks to our plan, glad to be occupied with logistics. Planning was what I did best. I liked order. I liked to be in control, and the last twenty-four hours I'd felt relegated to the backseat of my own car. I needed my foot back on the pedals, my own fingers wrapped around the wheel.

At the appointed hour, I called my mother. I made every effort to sound upbeat and not too concerned. She asked a few questions, all in the same zombie-like monotone she had affected after Dad died. I could feel her sinking beneath the surface again. My heart ached. How could I have done this to her so soon after Daddy's death?

The phone call to Mom exhausted me, and I slumped into the bed. I was unable to sleep. The thought that I might die from this continued to hover, but I would not allow it to land. Life unfolded as it needed to unfold. I believed I had been given the right conditions to help me overcome the particular obstacles that interfered with my connection to the Self and consequently communion with God. Believing that whatever came to be would be a gift freed me to focus on the present with greater stability and strength. To do so was my only hope. I was determined not to give in to self-pity and fear. It was not a viable option for a student of the Work.

Way back when I asked the question, What's the point of life? Gurudev's short answer was: to know God. His long answer was: to transcend the death of the physical body. The two answers are connected. Transcendence was accomplished through the development of a permanent and unwavering awareness of Self. It was this Self that could know God and be God, in much the same way a spark could become a flame. It was this Self that was inextinguishable, even while the body would, at some point, take its last breath. To the extent I understood anything about *the point*, it was only as a result of my personal efforts to observe the multi-faceted personality while at the same time holding awareness of the presence of Self and centering myself in it.

I was shifting uncomfortably on the bed, repositioning a pillow behind my back, when the nurse who had been there when Dr. Gardiner dropped his bomb returned to check on me.

"Who is going to do the biopsy?" I asked. "I don't know any doctors here. And it's my brain for god's sake."

"Look," she said, moving in closer. "All the neurosurgeons here are great, and I'm not supposed to say this, but of all the patients I've taken care of after brain surgery, Dr. Piepmeier's fared the best and recovered the fastest, hands down."

This, I thought, *is an important recommendation. She's on the inside. In the know.*

P-i-e-p-m-e-i-e-r. I wrote down his name on a paper napkin and slipped it in the night table drawer for safekeeping.

◆◆◆

The next day, Dr. Vives, the head of the neurological team came to see me. He extended his hand and offered a broad smile. I thought this was odd behavior for an agent of doom.

"I just came from the neurological team meeting. We viewed your scans and came up with a game plan," he said.

I braced myself.

"We recommend surgery to remove the 3-cm mass from the left parietal lobe of your brain. The mass is a meningioma and almost certainly benign."

Benign, I thought. *What is he saying? Doesn't he know about the bad brain tumor—the one Dr. Gardiner told me about?*

Dr. Vives continued. "We should be able to safely remove the entire tumor. If not, we will take out only what we can and follow up later with radiation treatments." I sat there stunned. His report was so different from Dr. Gardiner's. Who was I supposed to believe?

"Are you okay?" Dr. Vives asked. "This is good news you know."

I stared at him in confusion. Had he stumbled into my room by mistake? I wondered if my MRI had gotten mixed up with someone else's and questioned why he didn't seem to know what Dr. Gardiner knew. He didn't even mention that report. My heart raced.

"What about the biopsy?" I said, trying not to panic.

"Biopsy?"

"Yes, the biopsy. What about that? I thought you needed one to tell which kind of tumor I've got. And what about the hollow?" I continued, glancing down and reading from my notes. "I thought that's typical of the highly aggressive glioblastoma."

Dr. Vives looked at me as though I were speaking in tongues. "Where did you get all this from?"

I repeated the details of Dr. Gardiner's report. Dr. Vives listened without interrupting. His expression had turned pained.

"I'm so very sorry those possibilities were ever presented to you. It was unnecessary," he said. "We have absolutely no reason to suspect this is an aggressive cancer."

The tumor, he went on to explain, was pressing on the brain and causing seizures, so it had to come out. But in all likelihood, no further treatment would be necessary.

"You're going to be fine," he said.

"But the hollow… he said it's characteristic of a glioblastoma."

"The hollow is a necrosis formed of dead cells," Dr. Vives said.

My meningioma, it seemed, had been growing for many, many years. It was not surprising to him that at some time or other blood supply to a section of the mass had been cut off causing cell death and, thus, a hollow to form. It didn't mean the mass was a glioblastoma, he assured.

"And the biopsy? I don't need one?" I was almost too afraid to ask.

"When the tumor is removed, a sample will go to the pathology lab for analysis. You don't need any biopsy before that."

"Try to relax. You can go home for now. The Keppra you're taking will prevent further seizures and someone will call you to set up a date for the surgery."

Dr. Vives had been assigned to be my surgeon. I squirmed and looked away from him. Perhaps he sensed my discomfort because he quickly added that of course I could use another doctor if I preferred. Dr. Vives had been so nice to me, and this was so awkward. But hell, my brain was at stake.

"A few people I know recommended Dr. Piepmeier and I thought I might like to have him do the surgery."

"That's fine," he said. "I'll see if I can track him down and have him stop in before you go home."

After Dr. Vives left, I went over his words mining them for hidden meaning. Was it safe to believe him? He said he was the head of the neurological team. So then, who was Dr. Gardiner? I couldn't remember him telling me his title or department. And, what was the source of his report yesterday if the team hadn't met until this morning? Why didn't Dr. Gardiner know benign tumors can have hollows, too? Highly aggressive glioblastoma, he had said. I doubted I would ever get those three words out of my mind. They had burned, like a brand, into the surface of my injured brain.

As I replayed my conversation with Dr. Vives yet again, it became clear he, the head of the neurological team, and not Dr. Gardiner, was the one with the straight scoop. Benign. I loved that word. I went limp, sinking into the bed, my breathing slowing to a relaxed even tempo. I felt very tired, too tired even to call Andy, although I knew I should do so right away. I wanted to rest, to savor the sweet taste of relief a little while longer. I knew there would still be brain surgery, but thank god it wouldn't be tomorrow.

Not tomorrow! I thought, lunging for the phone to call my brother It took several rings for him to answer the call. I waited while he turned down the radio and switched his cell phone to speaker.

"Don't come," I said. "I'm not having a biopsy. The tumor is benign. Surgery will be later on, not now, so go home."

"What about everything they told you yesterday?" He sounded as confused as I had been.

I couldn't go into it again. Not then. I still had to call Andy, and he would need to hear all the details. I told Matt I'd fill him in later. For now, he should tell Mom the good news and go back home. It was too soon for them to come up. There would be time for that later.

Again, Andy picked up on the first ring. He sounded drained.

"Good news. I can go home," I said, before relaying every detail of my meeting with Dr. Vives.

Andy was relieved, but he too was upset at Dr. Gardiner for jumping the gun and alarming us with his unauthorized and erroneous report. I could tell, though, that in a matter of seconds Andy was already putting that behind him: the future was looking more positive, it was time to move on. But I couldn't. Something inside of me had been shattered by Dr.

Gardiner's words. Reassembling all the pieces was not going to be so easy.

There is a parable of a simple Jew who had a bad habit of telling tales and spreading rumors. One day, elaborating on a bit of gossip, he slandered the rabbi of the village, causing an uproar and damaging the rabbi's reputation. Later, he realized the wrong he had done and, feeling remorse, he went to the rabbi to ask forgiveness.

"I will do anything to make amends," he said.

The rabbi told him to go home, gather all the feather pillows in the house and then cut them open and scatter the feathers to the wind. The Jew thought this request was a little *meshugah*—crazy—but it was a simple enough task, and wanting very much to be forgiven, he did as the rabbi asked. His mission completed, he returned and reported he had done exactly as instructed.

"Good," said the rabbi. "Now, go and gather up all the feathers."

"But that's impossible! The wind has blown them far and wide."

"Just so," said the rabbi. "You can no more make amends for the damage your words have done than you can collect the feathers that have scattered in the wind."

Highly. Aggressive. Glioblastoma. Three irretrievable words. Damage that could not be undone.

♦♦♦

A tall, balding man with kind eyes and ruddy cheeks entered my hospital room and introduced himself as Dr. Joseph Piepmeier.

"I understand you would like me to do your surgery," he said. "You know, Dr. Vives is an excellent surgeon. You couldn't be in better hands."

I liked humility in a doctor, and my preference for Dr. Piepmeier only intensified.

"I'm sure he is, but it's my brain, and I think I'd be more comfortable if you would do the surgery."

Dr. Piepmeier smiled, said he would be happy to, and let me know his office would call to make the arrangements. I felt relieved, as though a first hurdle had been negotiated successfully.

Several hours later Andy arrived to pick me up and bring me home. Dr. Vives had said I could leave whenever I was ready, but I had told Andy he might as well wait until after work to come and get me, and this time I meant it. I wasn't ready to leave, to give Andy my attention, to answer questions, to talk at all. I was so exhausted, emotionally and physically. I craved a few hours of sleep before going home and facing whatever lay ahead. Content in the knowledge I could leave whenever I wanted, I took the opportunity to press pause, putting off the inevitable for at least a little while longer.

It was already dark by the time Andy arrived to break me out of that faceless factory of a hospital. I was free, but I felt more like a prisoner out on parole. I had been granted a temporary reprieve, but I would be back. Surgery awaited.

The cold slapped me in the face as we passed through the same revolving doors that had swept me in two long nights before. I clung to Andy's hand but didn't say much as we walked to the car. I felt shaky, subdued and somber, painted every shade of gray like the streets of New Haven.

"Do you want to go straight home?" Andy asked.

I didn't. I was hungry and didn't want to have to start fixing anything, if there was even anything to fix. It felt like a long time since I'd opened the door to my own refrigerator.

Andy seemed nervous. I couldn't blame him. I'd hardly spoken. He asked me where I would like to eat, and I said anywhere, I didn't care. He drove over to one of our favorite restaurants in New Haven. The building was an old time diner, all shiny aluminum with large plate glass windows.

Inside was a counter, stools, and a handful of tables. One would never expect the cuisine to be Indian—but it was.

At dinner I relaxed. It felt good to be in a familiar place, one that was part of what I had already come to think of as my "old life," the one before the diagnosis. Andy relaxed too. We talked about anything but the tumor and the upcoming surgery. We pretended to be an ordinary couple out for dinner on an ordinary night. It was at once tiring and a great relief.

Four

The first morning back home I had trouble waking up and arose in a stupor. Walking from the living room to the dining room I had difficulty navigating the few stairs that separated the two. I could not judge the distance between the steps. There was no banister and I wobbled precariously.

"Why do you keep pressing on your ear?" Andy said.

"It's been ringing. Really loud, more like a whine. Since yesterday. Do you think it's because of the tumor?"

Andy shrugged. "Could be anxiety," he said, offering it up as a more palatable explanation.

At the breakfast table, I stared at my cereal, stymied by the complex series of movements required to spoon the crinkled flakes out of the bowl. I had yet to learn about Gerstmann's Syndrome, a disorder caused by parietal lobe lesions. It explained both why I was confusing right and left and my occasional and alarming inability to recognize my own hand and fingers.

When I was a kid, my father had suffered a head injury in an auto accident. It left him with all his words, but they were in a jumble. I remembered one night sitting at the dinner table when he pointed to a glass bottle and asked me to "pass the football."

"Ketchup," I said. "Daddy, it's ketchup not football."

His face darkened, his lips tightened, and brow furrowed. The expression scared me. Even at nine I could see he was confounded and frustrated, just as I was now.

Andy was getting ready to leave for work, and I dreaded being left home alone all day. I was afraid, but I had no reason to ask him to stay. At least no reason I deemed legitimate. I wasn't sick, I wasn't in pain, and I'd been released from the hospital with only one restriction, no driving. There were spiritual principles I could have embraced and relaxation techniques I could have employed, but I did neither. I was spiraling out of control. Why couldn't I get it together?

Andy had been watching me with concern and once again called our brother-in-law for advice. Rich wasn't at home, but Debbie was.

"She's disoriented and having trouble with the steps," Andy said. "Is that normal? I mean, normal for now?"

Debbie was more than a little concerned. It didn't matter if it was normal for now or not. It was what it was, and she didn't think I should be left alone. And she is a nurse. She would know, right?

"She could have another seizure," Debbie said. "What if she falls, gets hurt, can't get up? Someone needs to be with her. Call Dad."

My in-laws, Selig and Juliet, lived in Fairfield, a few towns away. Selig agreed to come over and stay with me. I knew it would be at least an hour before he got to our house, but I told Andy he shouldn't wait. I promised to stay put on the recliner in the living room. Leaving the front door unlocked for his father, Andy left without protest, and I sat down disappointed that he had. I was sitting between two stools. I wasn't effectively dealing with my fear and stress, but neither was I willing to admit to it and accept it. That left me in the impossible position of wanting comfort, refusing to ask for it, and nursing resentment when it wasn't forthcoming.

When Selig arrived, I felt embarrassed. The panicked self had been replaced by a calmer more rational adult me who was too old for a babysitter. We talked and read, and I made us lunch. Afterwards, since it was on the mild side for December, I suggested we take a walk. At eighty-two, Selig was still tall, strapping and fit. His black hair was thinning and only peppered with gray. He liked to walk and so did I, but

My Father the Fish

mostly I didn't want him to be bored. It was bad enough he had to cancel whatever he had planned for the day to stay with me. I felt guilty, suspecting my unsteadiness and disorientation that morning were, at least in part, symptoms of anxiety and not the work of the meningioma's assault on my brain. Debbie had become alarmed unnecessarily, and my terrified self had gotten what it wanted—not to be left alone in the house all day. Selig and I walked for almost an hour. By the time we got back it was after 3 p.m. I suggested he go home while it was still light out and before traffic picked up. He made a weak show of protest, but it was clear he was ready to leave. And I wanted him to go. I was so tired. I assured him I'd be fine; I was going to nap. He gave me a bear hug and a sloppy kiss good-bye.

I locked the door, headed into the den, and collapsed on the couch. I fell into a deep sleep. I was awakened an hour later by the phone ringing. Again, I had trouble rousing myself, and I stumbled as I reached for the receiver. It was my friend Anneke.

I was disoriented, and I stuttered and shivered and fumbled for words. Anneke was concerned and had me call Andy on my cell phone while she stayed connected on the landline.

"Anneke says my spee---eech is very odd," "She--she thinks you shh--should come home." Andy asked where his dad was and when I told him I had sent him home, he got very agitated.

"Go sit down," he said. "I'm on my way."

I told Anneke good-bye and lay down again to wait. A short while later there was a knock at the door. Opening it, I was surprised to see our neighbor Henry.

"Hi," I said. "What's up?"

Henry stared at me, confused, like someone trying to work out a puzzle when he didn't have all the pieces.

"Don't *you* know?" he asked. "Andy called. He asked me to come over right away. To stay put until he got here."

God, I thought. *Andy didn't explain? He must have been really worried to have called Henry*—a good neighbor but not a close friend. I wondered how many numbers Andy had dialed before reaching someone at home in the late afternoon. Maybe he thought I was having a seizure or a stroke. My speech had been strange, but what Anneke was hearing for the first time—my stutter and difficulty in finding words and constructing sentences, and transposition of sounds—was a problem that had surfaced on occasion for months. Dr. Piepmeier said it was a symptom of conduction aphasia, yet another disorder resulting from the specific location of the tumor on my brain.

Though somewhat embarrassed, I was relieved to have another person in the house. And Henry was a dermatologist—not exactly an expert on brains but at least a doctor. I waited while he unbundled himself, dropping his parka and scarf on the bench, and then led him into the living room. He fidgeted and looked everywhere but at me. This was par for the course with Henry. Maybe with people he knew better he was more relaxed, but back then, with me, he seemed ill at ease.

Henry didn't react when I told him I had a brain tumor. If I'd said "warts" perhaps he'd have shown more interest. Or maybe he didn't want to invade my privacy any more than he felt he already had.

"I've been having seizures. The way I sounded when I called Andy, I guess he got scared. I'm sorry he didn't explain. But my speech is ok now, right?"

"I guess," Henry said with a shrug.

It was not only my speech that had improved since I hung up with Anneke. I was no longer disoriented. Although I had been very tired and had insisted Selig leave when he did, I was still afraid of being left alone. It wasn't just fear of a seizure, after all I'd already driven though Flatland and stood frozen like a statue with more puzzlement than fear. It was the knowledge of the tumor's reality that terrified me, and I didn't want to be alone with that knowledge in my head. As soon as Andy told me he was coming home I began to relax.

Henry and I spent an awkward half hour making small talk. Over the years, we had had dinner with Henry and his family a handful of times, but we had never developed much of a friendship beyond that. I was so glad when I heard Andy coming through the front door.

That evening I cried. My life had been turned upside down. I had plunged into Flatland, and I had been diagnosed with a brain tumor. What would be next? All I knew was I didn't want to be alone should new symptoms emerge or seizures recur. And the family didn't think it was safe anyway—at least not until it was certain the pills I was taking had brought the seizures under control. Why hadn't the hospital told me I shouldn't be left alone? "Don't drive" was the only instruction on the discharge papers. *First Dr. Gardiner, now this*, I thought. How could I put my life in the hands of a bunch of doctors who didn't communicate with each other and didn't relay important information to me? I had never been so scared in my life.

The next day, Andy worked from home.

Sunday, seven days after my wild ride on the Merritt Parkway, we returned to the hospital. Dr. Piepmeier had scheduled me for another MRI. This one would provide information he needed to plan the surgery, which had yet to be scheduled. A heavy wet snow fell, blanketing the roads in no time. They were slippery, and my hand flew up to the dashboard again and again in fearful anticipation of a skid. Andy told me to close my eyes and relax, and I did close my eyes, but I couldn't relax. I had visions of a horrendous wreck with me pinned beneath a burning car. I laughed at myself. How absurd to be conjuring improbable visions of death by car crash when I was facing brain surgery. But fear is fear and once catalyzed it is perfectly comfortable with a moving target.

We arrived and made our way through the basement of the hospital. Safety requirements meant radiology was often situated below ground level. The hallways were deserted. The waiting room, empty. A couple with an infant stood by the doorway speaking to a doctor about rescheduling the baby's tests. I hoped I wouldn't have to wait long. I wanted to get this over with. We had just gotten our coats off when a technician came for us. She explained Andy couldn't stay with me, but he could sit with her and he'd be able to see and hear me. I felt better knowing Andy would be keeping watch during the forty-five minutes I would lay on my back, immobile and trapped, inside the chamber. I took one last look at him before the technician had me lay down on the platform, took my glasses, placed ear plugs in my ears and a call button in my hand. She flipped a switch and the platform slid into the machine.

"Relax," she said. "We're not starting yet." She needed to do a sound check to make sure she and Andy could hear me, and I could hear them. They retreated into the small room from which she would control the scan. A large glass window afforded them a clear view of the MRI apparatus.

"Lorri, can you hear me?" she asked.

I could.

"Andy, you won't leave, will you?" I said. "I mean not at all. Not even to go to the bathroom."

Andy assured me he wouldn't budge, and with that she started the scan. At first there were a lot of clicking sounds, but very soon the clanging and banging began. In an effort to relax, I turned my attention to my breath. With my ears plugged against the din of the machine, the sound of my breathing was amplified. In and out. In and out. I drifted with my breath and imagined I was snorkeling. I used to snorkel often when I lived in Maui. Underwater, the sound of my breath would fill my head. The slow even rhythm was as hypnotic now as it was then.

Ever so softly, I began to sing. *Gam ki eilech, bigeh tzalmavet lo irrah ra ki atah imadee.* The tune was Neshama Carlebach's. The words were a verse from the 23rd Psalm, the only verse I knew by heart. Like a mantra, I chanted it over and over. The constant jabbering that usually filled my mind quieted down. After many repetitions the chant trailed off, and into the clabbering din of the MRI I whispered the verse in English: "Though I walk in the valley overshadowed by death, I will fear no evil for You are with me."

The words set off an explosion, reverberating in my skull, bouncing off bone, and slamming into my chest. I knew then, with unshakeable certainty, I was not, and never had been, alone. God's compassion extended to me. I was a part of, and not separate from, that greater Presence. The realization was stunning, for despite all my meditations focused on God within, and my picturing of the Self, (the one with the capital "S"), as a metaphorical finger of the hand of God reaching down through the heavens into the essence of me, in practice I had still always put God somewhere outside myself. For thirty years I'd been talking the talk but not walking it.

And there was more. I understood, not just in my rational mind but in the whole of me, that I had been living in death's shadow ever since I took my first breath. The brain tumor hadn't cast me into that valley. In sickness or in health, death always lingered in wait. It was not separate from life, it was part of it. I found that thought oddly comforting. From the moment of diagnosis, the tumor had taken on enormous import, a terrifying, looming presence, a stick of dynamite with a lit fuse. But the psalm had snuffed the flame. The tumor was just another way death cast its shadow. Nothing special. Nothing extraordinary. Nothing to be feared.

"OK. That's it. We're done," the technician said.

In another moment the platform conveyed me feet first out of the imaging chamber. I felt groggy and didn't attempt to sit up. The technician removed the plugs from my ears and extended her arm to help me.

"You were singing gam ki eilech," Andy said. "Almost the whole time."

I stared at him. I didn't feel all there. My world had changed—radically. I had, for a brief time, known God as inseparable from the Self within me. When I said "I will fear no evil for You are with me," I felt as though God was companioning God's own reflection in the Self.

The technician walked Andy and me out to the waiting room. I leaned against the wall. My head whirled, and I slid down to the floor and closed my eyes. A couple of nurses rushed over, raised me up off the floor, and laid me down on a gurney. Fingers pressed into my wrist, and a cuff tightened around my bicep. My normally low blood pressure had spiked to 147/75. A voice called out, "Get the on-duty doc in here. Stat!" Was I the cause of the commotion? I did feel strange, weak, as though all the fuel had been drained from my tank. The doctor arrived, checked me out, and left me to rest on the gurney. After ten minutes or so the whirling passed, Andy helped me up, and we headed for home. The snowstorm no longer fazed me. I eyed the icy road with detached disinterest. For the time being, at least, I was at peace living in the shadow of death.

Five

It was Tuesday, a few days after the MRI, and I wanted to head to my class at The Towers, the assisted living residence where I taught *Let it Shine*, a weekly sage-ing program. I had a lesson plan already prepared. It was the one I would have followed the past week had I not been otherwise engaged in the neurology wing of Yale New Haven. I hoped a return to my normal routine would have a stabilizing effect. Besides, I looked forward to seeing the octa- and nonagenarians I had developed close ties to during my teaching internship. Then, I had worried that since I was only fifty-four, they wouldn't take me seriously. What, after all, could I know about getting old? Now I was, in some ways, walking in their shoes, and I saw that as a gift. I was better equipped than ever to lead them in this sage-ing work.

I understood firsthand what it meant to be bereft of energy, to have to give up my car keys, and to be unable to keep my focus at times. I had an opportunity here to model the skills for coping with illness and facing mortality, and I felt a responsibility to do it well. Buoyed by this resolve, I took refuge in a bit of magical thinking: I *would* recover. After all, why would the universe throw this gift my way, if I was not going to have the opportunity to use it.

My mother-in-law, Juliet, offered to pick me up and drive me to The Towers. She was a great blessing in my life, my second mother. I could always depend upon her for recipes and household tips, second opinions on kitchen tile or paint colors, and a listening ear. She had been a beautiful young woman and that beauty remained, though muted and softened by the years. Though on the short side, she stood tall, and had a spry step. I could relax with her, knowing she could hold her own.

The Towers, two connected multistory brick apartment buildings in downtown New Haven, are home to more than three hundred older adults. A growing majority are eighty-five years old or older. Aides assist some residents, and others live independently. I met with my group in the communal dining room. Large plate glass windows looked out over the parking lot and a stone patio that would be sprinkled with lawn chairs and tables with broad-striped umbrellas come summer. Photographs, pastels, and paintings created by residents in art classes hung on the walls.

When Juliet and I arrived, the fifteen or so residents who attended my program each week were already assembled around a long table. Walkers, some spare economy models, others replete with handbrakes, a vinyl-covered seat, and a hanging basket for sundries—were abandoned helter-skelter, blocking our path. Ellsworth, at seventy-something, the youngest member of the group and always the gentleman, jumped up to clear the way for us. African-American, rail thin, and smartly dressed in dark slacks and a pressed oxford-cloth shirt, Ellsworth was an active member of The Towers community. He led chair exercise, played Wii golf, and participated in Yiddish class. Lou, Sid, and Harold, first-generation Jewish Americans in their nineties, were engaged in a heated discussion about the previous night's pinochle game. Harold's age hadn't curbed his penchant for the ladies. While I was getting myself settled, he turned to Ruth and made a somewhat off-color remark about the cut of her jib. Ruth, elegantly dressed and coifed, bantered back. Harold responded in Yiddish, and Ellsworth snickered.

I sat down at the head of the table and rummaged in my bag for my lesson plan. It was all I could do not to begin by blurting out: "I have a brain tumor." I glanced at my outline, up at the group, and then down again. I didn't have it in me to talk about "Creating Sacred Space." I turned my notes face down and said, "Let's talk about prayer." It was on my mind—had been ever since my experience in the MRI on Sunday. I couldn't think of anything else. I had inadvertently and without expectation beckoned to God to take a step closer, and it seemed God had. What did that mean? I was still struggling to reconcile my understanding of a transcendent God with that of the immanent "God within." The "Ah-ha" experience of Sunday was already fading. I needed to work through this on my own, to consolidate what I learned in that moment of grace.

Contradictions didn't phase me, or I should say "apparent" contradictions. Often, I'd found disagreements and discrepancies were reconciled when viewed from a high enough perspective. I thought again of my mental image of the hand of God, waggling fingers down through the heavens and piercing the clouds. From below, there appeared to be five separate and discreet fingers; from above, I saw they were but extensions of the one hand.

When God was the subject, transcendence and immanence were not so much opposites, as two halves of a whole. Was there a role for prayer? Who does the praying?

"Raise your hand if you have ever prayed," I said, and waited. "C'mon, that's not a hard question…"

One by one hands went up. Each week it was the same story. They needed time to settle in, to get comfortable with each other, before they would open up.

Gert expectantly looked from side to side as if she had something to say but hoped someone else would speak first. Then, "What do you mean by prayer?" she asked. "Not everyone means the same thing."

"Good point. What do *you* mean by prayer?"

Harold pounced on that one before Gert could formulate an answer. "The Torah says pray three times a day. And I have. My whole life. Every page in the siddur."

Ruth chimed in. "I don't think prayer has to be from a

prayer book. It can be your own words." Harold gave her a look that said my way or the highway, and Ruth rolled her eyes.

More hands went up, more opinions ventured.

"It can be meditation."

"Or gospel. A singing prayer."

"If you're talking to God, that's praying."

"God doesn't listen. Look at the Holocaust and you tell me God listens! What prayers did God hear then?"

Was God in fact listening...ever? I hadn't thought so. The God I had envisioned for many years was distant and dispassionate and not the least bit interested in the trials, joys or tribulations of any one individual who walked this earth. God, I believed, took about as much notice of me as I took of a single one of my liver cells. Yet, my unexpected foray into prayer within the confines of the MRI machine had not been my first. When I was nineteen, I had talked to God. God hadn't talked back, but I had believed God was listening.

This one-sided conversation took place after a miserable freshman year at SUNY New Paltz. I had transferred to William Smith College thinking all would be right with my world if only I were at a school whose students were more often to be found in the library, nose in the books, than sprawled in the halls of the dorm, downed-out on Quaaludes. Though William Smith, with its ivy-covered walls, excellent faculty, and rigorous academics, offered everything I thought I wanted from a university, I fared no better than I had the prior year at New Paltz. I was very depressed. I felt dead inside, and there was nothing I could point to that would explain why. I hardly slept and subsisted largely on ice cream. It was one of the few cafeteria offerings that would slide down over the perpetual lump in my throat. One night my roommate returned from the library to find me lying in bed shaking. I couldn't, or wouldn't, respond to her, so she called security and they hauled me off to the infirmary. The nurse prescribed "a rest" and called my parents. They arranged a plane ticket to bring me home for a long weekend of TLC. I didn't return to school.

Several weeks later, I lay corpse-like in the bedroom I'd grown up in. I felt no better than I had at school despite the antidepressants circulating in my blood stream and the dozen or so psychotherapy visits under my belt. I stared up at the whorls of sand-paint on the ceiling. I thought a lot about dying. I was not suicidal, it was just that being dead seemed to be a better option than continuing to live feeling the way I did.

"I can't take this anymore," I said aloud, my words filling the empty room. Then, to my own surprise, I prayed the only prayer I knew: *The Lord's Prayer*. It was the national anthem of Dad's Alcoholic's Anonymous group. Growing up, AA was the closest thing we had to religion in my home, and I had learned this prayer when I attended Alateen, the self-help program for children of alcoholics. All those years when I had risen from my seat to recite it at Alateen meetings, I had never thought of it as praying, but more like standing for the pledge of allegiance—something one did when called upon to do so. But that night, this prayer, which I repeated out loud over and over, was a prayer of my heart. "Our Father, who art in heaven, hallowed be thy name. Thy kingdom come, thy will be done, on earth as it is in heaven…" I had little to no relationship to the words which for me evoked an image of a hoary headed man with flowing beard peering down from his celestial throne. It was a depiction reminiscent of illustrations in my childhood *Golden Book of Bible Stories*, and it did not portray a God I could believe in. Still, I prayed, fueled by a faint hope that maybe there was help for me in a direction I had not considered looking before.

Help did come, though precisely "how" was a mystery. Perhaps it was the focused repetition of the prayer that altered my consciousness and opened the door to a modicum of peace. I felt as though I were floating up near the ceiling, looking down at my body lying on the bed, lips moving in prayer. Surrendering to "Our Father who art in Heaven," I was released from that wasted body and tormented soul. I experienced what I would later come to understand as a taste of the separation of one's Self, the God with-in, from the many clingy selves of personality. The relief I felt wasn't permanent, but that night was a turning point. I began the steep climb out of the pit of depression.

Had my "Our Fathers" and "Gam ki eilechs" actually been heard? And if so, by whom—the God transcendent or God immanent? Should I direct my prayers up or in? If, as I believed, God was infinite and omniscient, then it stood to reason that God knew my Self as God knew Itself, for my Self existed within God. There was no other place to be. Immanent and transcendent, God could be both a loving companion and an impersonal force. There was no contradiction here, only an expanding perspective.

And if I prayed, what kind of result could I hope for? The rabbis said, God hears every prayer, only sometimes the answer is "No." Would that explanation have to do, or was there more to the story?

There was an uncomfortable shuffle and shift around the table and a low rumble that the word "Holocaust" always elicits from this group of mostly Jewish elders.

"Well what about that, does God listen or not?" Agnes said, with a tap tap of her cane, followed by mumbled yeas and nays from her cohorts around the table.

Jolted back from my own meandering, I scrambled to recover the thread of discussion where I had lost it.

"What do you think? Who hasn't spoken yet? Does God hear our prayers? If not, then who are you talking to when you pray, and what are you hoping for as a result?"

I was surprised to hear so many varied points of view, approaches, and reasons for praying in the first place. While some answers were pat, many were thoughtful—and some suggested struggle. The group was caught up in the topic, and I was relieved. I needed to hear it discussed. I had so many questions of my own. When the volleying dwindled to a lull, I took my turn.

"I wasn't here last week because I was in the hospital. I have a brain tumor, but I'll be fine. It's benign."

"What did she say?" Lillian asked, fiddling with her hearing aide.

"Brain tumor," Gert answered, pointing to her head. "She says she has a brain tumor."

I surveyed the anxious faces and repeated, "I'll be fine. I'll need to take some time off for surgery. But not yet."

Questions hurdled at me: Did you get a second opinion? Do they know what caused it? Are you in pain? I waved off their questions. I wanted to get back to talking about prayer, and in a few minutes we would have to end, so they could go to lunch.

"I've got a story," I said, and the folks quieted and settled into their chairs. "Last week, I was in the middle of getting an MRI when, out of the blue, I began reciting a psalm. I hadn't even realized at first that I was praying. But when it was over, and the tech slid me out and helped me up, I knew God had been listening. I wasn't alone."

There was a hush. No one commented on my story. Perhaps it made them uncomfortable, I didn't know. I left amidst a volley of promises that they would pray for my complete recovery. I was bolstered by their well-wishing. I felt my whole team behind me, cheering me on. I was not disappointed when no one asked me what I meant when I said God could hear my prayers. Had they, I still would not have had an answer. Yet, I knew it to be true. Sometimes we can know in our gut what we can't explain.

On the first road trip I ever took with Andy he had tried to teach me the *Traveler's Prayer*. I had rolled my eyes finding it hard to believe he went in for such superstitious mojo. Did he really think a prayer to God was what it took to protect us at 70 mph on I-75? Where was God when a tire blew, landing my father in a coma and my mother in a wheelchair? And what about when the drunk careened head-on into my friend Marcia's car? If she had said a little prayer, would God have been listening? Would the Fates have swayed in a different direction?

Andy pushed and cajoled, and I was the new girlfriend already daydreaming about becoming his wife. *Aim to please* was that girl's unconscious motto, so I gave in, if half-heartedly. I wouldn't learn all the Hebrew, but after reciting the traditional opener, *B'shem Adonai, Elohei Yisrael*—In the name of our Lord, God of Israel—I offered up my very own, very loose translation. It went like this: "May we go in peace, may we come in peace, may all our travels be in peace. And may we be protected along the way from lions and tigers and bears, deer, turkey, coyote and all manner of wildlife, road hazards, crazy drivers, and our own inattention." With a nod to Andy, I ended my short request with the formulaic closer: "With *chain* (grace), *chesed* (compassion), and *rachamin* (mercy), Amen."

Andy had accepted my version, and over time it became our version. I guessed he thought it was better than nothing. I recited it on our trips together and sometimes even when I was travelling alone. Two car accidents had affected my life profoundly, and repeating this makeshift prayer subdued the fear that too often tightened around my chest. I said the words, but I had never considered them as an address to God. I had held that my chant was a bit of magic like knocking on wood—something to do in case there really was some hoodoo at work in the universe. Yet, when I said, "may we be protected along the way...," wasn't it an acknow-ledgment that a safe outcome was not, ultimately, in my hands, and if not, then in whose hands was it? This letting go of control had relieved me of an enormous burden. It let me breathe freer. Despite my assertions to the contrary, I had, in fact, been praying all along. My incantation may have sounded like mojo, but it presumed a holy listener as witness.

I continued to struggle with what it meant for God to hear my prayers. And, if I wasn't alone, if God was always with me, who was the "me" God was with? Was it "me" at all?

I knew from many years of practice at paying attention to and analyzing my thoughts and feelings that I was inconsistent and mercurial. What made me angry in one moment could make me laugh in another. I was capable of both bumbling around like a blithering idiot and running a board meeting with the utmost confidence. My life, *The Story of Lorri*, was like a Broadway show that I not only starred in, but played all the roles. Each character in the play had her own tics and traits, doubts and dreams, and each went by the name, Lorri. To keep all these Lorri's straight in my mind, I assigned a nickname that in someway personified the predominant attitude or behavior of the particular character. During any one scene, Bitch, Store Manager, File Clerk, Terrified Child, or King Tut might make an appearance. The one I called The Watcher was a special member of the cast. She did a little acting, but her most important role was that of director. She grew into that role through holding a spiritual aim. She wanted to know God, and as such her thoughts and actions were not a result of passing whims—the push and pull of desires and aversions—but were guided by the principles of the Work to which she held fast.

The Watcher sat in the balcony from where she had a broader perspective of the action on the stage. She watched the characters deliver their lines, taking note of their affectations, listening to their lies and self-deceptions, justifications, histrionics, and irrational thoughts—and she did so without flinching—re-directing the action, when necessary, to steer the character onto a path defined by spiritual principles. Not all the "Lorri's" portrayed such problematic characters, some were thoughtful, upstanding, caring folk who wreaked no havoc, even did good. The Watcher watched them too, but didn't interfere. Even though they weren't walking the path, they were at least headed in a complementary direction.

The Watcher was steeped in the teachings of The Work. She never forgot that apart from the many little selves playing a role in *The Story of Lorri*, there was *the* Self, with a capital S. It alone was eternal and unchanging. It witnessed, but never acted. When the final curtain came down scripts would be shelved, costumes stowed, and all little selves would leave the theatre. Only the Self would remain.

When I was in the MRI chanting, and I had the epiphany that I was never alone, that God was with me, aware of me, listening to me, I didn't for a minute think it was any of those little selves keeping close company with God. No, it was the Self, not any member of the cast not even the Watcher. The Self was the one communing with God. When it "spoke," God "heard," as one hears one's own innermost thoughts.

◆ ◆ ◆

Juliet delivered me home from The Towers and sat down to a cup of tea, while I collapsed on the couch wanting to call it a day. I was exhausted and had only a couple of hours to rest up before my appointment with Dr. Piepmeier. As tired as I was, I was also anxious to have this meeting that had been described as the opportunity for me to ask all my questions about the surgery. At the conclusion of the meeting I was expected to sign the consent forms. Without the signed forms in hand, they couldn't schedule the surgery, and I wanted to have the operation as soon as possible so I could get my life back on track.

I had had surgery once before. I knew the forms would spell out all the things that could go wrong. I also knew I would read every word before signing, and the horrific warnings would scare the pants off me. I reminded myself the forms were aimed at protecting the hospital from liability, and while all the worst-case scenarios were possible, they were not likely. In any event, as I had noted a few days earlier, life came with no guarantees. I could die in a car accident before even reaching the operating table.

Andy's sister Debbie was coming down from Boston to drive me to the appointment. Andy had gone into work. He would meet us there. Nurse Debbie was not one to keep quiet about anything. I knew she would have my back. When my father-in-law had undergone cancer treatment, I had seen Debbie in action. She picked up on mistakes in medication, alerted the nurses to changes in condition, and made suggestions for keeping her dad more comfortable. Put her in a hospital, her natural habitat, and she was like a tiger in the jungle: savvy, keen, and decisive. I knew I could count on her to ask important questions that might not occur to me or to pick up on anything that didn't sound right.

Both Andy and Debbie were delayed by heavy traffic. To save Debbie the backtracking to my house, Juliet drove me to a parking lot near Debbie's highway exit. She sat in her car, but I got out and paced, straining my neck in the direction Debbie would be coming from. When Debbie did arrive, I wouldn't let her get out of her car. I jumped right into the passenger seat. Juliet greeted her daughter through the open window and then headed home, while Debbie and I took off for New Haven.

Debbie talked, I only half listened. I was busy checking my watch every minute or so, while she drove through the unfamiliar streets without hesitation, the way she did everything. Debbie and Andy looked like brother and sister, with their almost black hair and their mother's slightly almond shaped eyes, but they couldn't be more different in personality. Debbie stepped to the front of the line and filled every room she entered, while Andy quietly stepped back to make room for others. In that moment, I welcomed her natural inclination to take charge and plow through.

Andy called to let us know his whereabouts. "There's a lot of traffic," Andy said. "But I should still be on time."

"There's always traffic, you should have left earlier. You should have come home and picked me up yourself."

"Listen," Andy said, "If you get there before me and the doctor calls you in, go ahead, and I'll come in as soon as I arrive."

"You just don't get it!" I said. This was neither the first nor the last time I would feel let down by Andy.

Running late was par for the course with him, and the catalyst for a painful pattern in our relationship. At least, painful for me. There had been countless times when I had been infuriated by Andy's inattention to the passage of time. We lived in parallel universes. "Why aren't you ready? The play starts at 2:30 and we said we would leave by 2 p.m.!" Without any sense of urgency, he would finish reading an email, put on his shoes and coat, gather up his keys and tell me to relax, we'd be there on time. It galled me no end that we always were. Always. It was more suffering I caused myself, and here I was doing it again.

Andy arrived at the Yale School of Medicine building on Cedar Street moments after we did. *Figures*, I thought, but any residual annoyance was dwarfed by my relief at seeing him.

I was grateful that our meeting was not taking place in the hospital. Walking into a university building was the sort of thing I'd done many times before—to take a class, meet with a professor, or hear a lecture.

We did not have to wait long before the receptionist ushered us into a small narrow examining room. Bookshelves packed with medical texts lined the walls. A Naugahyde examining table took up a third of the space, and I sat on it after Andy and Debbie took the only two chairs. The wall opposite me was glass from waist to ceiling. I couldn't make out what was on the other side. I felt caged, like a lab rat. Before I could get up and peer through the glass Dr.

Piepmeier came through a door in that wall that separated light from darkness. His surgical nurse and an intern followed, wedging themselves in between the bookshelves and the exam table. A couple of more people and we'd be packed in like clowns in a Volkswagen. Introductions were made all around.

Dr. Piepmeier described the size and location of the tumor and reiterated his conviction that it was benign. Given the alternatives, this was good news, yet I failed to feel good about it. I asked for clarification as to the location of the left parietal lobe where the tumor was located, and Dr. Piepmeier responded by ushering us into the wide, dimly lit hallway lined with computers and other medical equipment. He directed our attention to a monitor perched on an eye-level workstation. The screen glowed in the darkness. Dr. Piepmeier struck a few keys and up came what looked like a kind of x-ray.

"This is an MRI of your brain. This here," Dr. Piepmeier said, pointing to the scan, "is the left parietal lobe. And this is the tumor."

Dr. Piepmeier pointed to a white splotch on the left side of the image I was coming to recognize as a brain. I stared at the splotch in confusion. Dr. Vives had told me "it's the size of a golf ball," and that was what I had been expecting it to look like—a symmetrical orb about an inch and a half in diameter. When I'd imagined the surgery, I'd pictured Dr. Piepmeier opening my skull like one would a small cabinet, reaching in to pluck out the "golf ball," then closing my head up again. But that was no golf ball in there. Though about the same size as one, it looked more like an amoeba with small tentacles, not like something that could be easily plucked out. This evidence of the tumor, right there in front of me in black and white, conveyed the reality of the diagnosis in a way that words had not. I had been keeping my anxiety in check since we had arrived for the appointment, but now my insides turned to jelly.

Dr. Piepmeier led us back into the small examining room and explained why, in my case, surgery was the safest and best choice. Other options, like gamma knife radiation, had been ruled out because of the size of the tumor. He explained the proximity of the meningioma to a major vein and an important nerve meant that it might not be possible to remove the entire mass, but he wouldn't know for sure until the surgery was in progress. He would not risk damage to the nerve. There was a small chance, he said, radiation treatments would be necessary, but again, that could not be known in advance of the surgery. I began to babble, asking question after question. I didn't comprehend a single answer.

"Explain again why I need the surgery?" I said. "If it's benign, why can't we leave it alone? Wouldn't gamma knife be safer? Could I just take medicine? Will I need radiation? The seizures have stopped, so maybe it will go away."

Dr. Piepmeier raised his hand to end my questioning. It was clear to him I was too anxious to understand my condition or the treatment options. He told me to reschedule an appointment for a later date.

Noooooooooooo, I wanted to scream. No more delays. I wanted the whole ordeal over with. I scrambled to salvage the meeting.

"Can I speak to you alone, please?" I said. I was desperate and willing to say anything—even to lie—if it would change Dr. Piepmeier's mind, and so I needed Andy and Debbie out of the room where they couldn't rat me out.

"The Nurse Lady," I said. "She can stay."

Everyone turned and stared at me. The *Nurse Lady?* What could I do? I couldn't remember her name. But I wanted her in the room. Somehow I felt she would be an ally against this doctor. I was as intimidated by him as I had been by the men in suits that surrounded me in my corporate life. After Andy, Debbie, and the intern left, I stated my case with conviction as though my life depended on it.

"I know I'm a little nervous," I said. "But I am very

My Father the Fish

intelligent. I can understand all this. Let me try again. Just explain it all one more time."

"Lorri," Dr. Piepmeier said. "Your anxiety is a greater and more immediate threat to your health than this tumor. It would be irresponsible on my part to allow you to sign consent forms in your present state of mind."

He scribbled the name of a psychiatrist on his pad and handed me the paper.

"Get some help. Then come back. Delaying the surgery for a few weeks, or even a couple of months, won't make any difference at all in the size of the tumor. And besides, Christmas is coming up and many on my staff will be on vacation through New Year's. I would rather wait until I have my full team with me, not fill-in staff."

And with that, he and the Nurse Lady said their good-byes and exited.

On the way home, Debbie drove alone, and I rode with Andy. I seethed in silence. I had been rejected by my own surgeon, deemed too neurotic to sign off on the surgery and ordered to see a psychiatrist. I had had a simple task in front of me: sign the consent forms and schedule a date for the surgery. I had failed.

"Tell Debbie to go back to Boston tonight," I said, while we idled at a traffic light. I wanted to be left alone. Maybe forever. "And your parents. Make sure they leave for Sanibel on Friday. I don't want them sticking around because of me." Andy reached across the car seat and took my hand. He stroked my fingers with his thumb, but I would not be consoled.

We arrived at home minutes before Debbie. Andy unlocked the house. I pushed passed him, headed straight into our bedroom, and shut the door. The room was a comfort to me, a refuge. I sat on the bed propping myself up against an assortment of quilted throw pillows. I could hear Andy and Debbie's muffled voices coming from the living room. I knew Andy wouldn't tell her to leave. No matter. I had our room to myself, and I needed to think.

Dr. Piepmeier is right. I can't continue like this. I thought. I had lost all perspective. My emotions were out of control, battering me, relentless wave after wave. It was useless to try and stop them, but I knew how to let them wash over me. As a little kid at Jones Beach, my dad had taught me to jump the waves as they rushed onto the shore. But sometimes when they were too big to jump; they would smack into me, drag me down, and whack me into the seabed. Enormous waves like that, he told me, I had to dive into the moment before they crested. He said if I offered no resistance I would find it was calm at the very center and the wave would deliver me gently to shore. The first time I did it was an act of faith, but Dad had been right. It worked every time.

The way to dive into the emotions that were wreaking havoc was to do what Gurudev had instructed me to do: call upon the Watcher, the one who would observe the ranting and raving with patience, compassion, and without self-judgment, knowing it was all passing experience and did not define who I was. The Watcher was a strong swimmer, willing and able to dive into the center of the wave where the chaos of all that was impermanent would wash over me.

I came to see Dr. Piepmeier's actions that afternoon in a different light. His move was brilliant. I had boarded a train that was barreling down the track and he had brought it to a screeching halt. He gave me a gift—time to come to terms with my diagnosis and what was to come. I wasn't just body parts to him, a brain with a tumor. I was a whole person with feelings and thoughts; when he sent me away he was considering all of me.

The turmoil and terror returned later that evening as it would return again and again. It was unpleasant, but not unexpected. I had no choice but to keep at it: keep thinking, keep relaxing the body, keep watching the whole show from that one still place inside. The goal was not to eradicate emotions, but to weaken the hold the emotions had on me by putting them in perspective; they were temporary, not a permanent fixture, not the Self.

I looked for comfort too. Wrapped in Andy's arms as we lay in bed, I whispered into the darkness. "Pray with me?"

Tightening his hold around me, Andy intoned the traditional Jewish bedtime prayer that called upon the angels Gavriel, Michael, Uriel, and Rifael to encircle me and the *Shekhina*, God's presence, to dwell above me. Between gentle kisses, he offered a *Mi sheberakh*, a prayer for my healing, and I was comforted. The demons that had been tormenting me slithered back from whence they had come and I drifted off to sleep.

In the morning I called my mother. Thank God for telephones, because talking to her helped me keep my head on straight. She was struggling herself since my dad died, but when I called her that day she rallied. She had a boatload of slogans from her years in Al-Anon, the program for spouses and other adult family members of alcoholics. *Put I over E*, she would say, meaning take the lead from your intellect and not your emotions. *This too shall pass. God never gives us more than we can handle. Accept the things you can not change. Change the things you can*, and on and on. It never felt like she was tossing out platitudes. Her little sayings were always pertinent in the moment, and they were easy to digest. She also never put her two cents in regarding decisions to be made about treatments or doctors. She listened, a good sounding board. My mother had had breast cancer many years before, and I never forgot her saying Daddy had offered her the very best kind of support by leaving her to make her own decisions. She must have remembered that, too, because she followed his lead to a tee. Mom encouraged me to see a psychologist. It will be good for you to talk with someone objective, she'd said, and she was right.

I knew a psychologist, Cheryl, from holiday celebrations

at Andy's *shul*—his synagogue. I called her and asked for a referral to a therapist. I did not want to call the psychiatrist Dr. Piepmeier had recommended. I had a low opinion of psychiatry. I'd seen a psychiatrist myself for a while when I was nineteen and struggling with depression. I'd also heard stories from friends. Too many of those shrinks were glorified drug pushers with a license to peddle, and that put me off. Cheryl gave me a couple of names, but it was too late to call anyone. No longer angry or self-hating, I joined Andy and Debbie for dinner. First thing the next morning, I reached Dr. Fountain. It would be a week before I got in to see her.

♦♦♦

New Haven was crowded at midday. No parking spots were available near Dr. Fountain's office, so Andy dropped me off and promised to pick me up in an hour. I headed inside and pushed the elevator button. The hallway was long. The carpet and the wall paint were not new. All the doors were the same, no glass and no signage except for suite numbers. I glanced again at the address scrawled on the yellow sticky note and located the door to her office, suite 1201. I walked into a narrow, windowless waiting room that served two doctors. A few chairs were pushed up against the white walls and magazines were fanned out atop a coffee table. There was no one else in the room, not even a receptionist. I sat down facing two closed doors. *Should I knock? On which door?* Neither was marked. I felt overwhelmed by the weight of even small decisions.

At exactly 11 a.m. a door swung open and an attractive, well-groomed woman of about sixty extended her hand and ushered me into the inner office. It was filled with light. Windows looked out to the street many stories below. The furniture was of a simple straight-line design. She offered me a chair and sat across from me. I had a note pad and an agenda. I had planned out in advance what I wanted to say and what I hoped to accomplish by seeing her: I needed to calm down, so Dr. Piepmeier would let me sign the consent form. Therapists don't come cheap, and I was not about to waste any of the time I was paying for. I got right down to business telling her about the brain tumor and the disaster I'd made of my visit to Dr. Piepmeier. Then I told her about the conversation with Dr. Gardiner.

"Listen," I said. "I don't for a minute think Dr. Gardiner had any malicious intent when he threw out the possibility of such a devastating diagnosis, but so what? The road to hell, as they say."

Dr. Gardiner knew the neurosurgical team hadn't reviewed my MRI, made a diagnosis or a treatment plan. So he had no business saying anything to me at all. "Whatever happened to, 'physician, first do no harm'?" I asked.

Dr. Fountain nodded and shifted in her seat, and I continued with my diatribe. I was angry—with Dr. Gardiner, Yale Medical School, and Yale New Haven Hospital. Why weren't they doing a better job teaching all the wannabe doctors that patients are more than just bodies? Whatever happened to empathy? I took a breath and sat back in my chair.

"That must have been very terrifying for you," she said. "I understand why you feel angry. Go on."

Dr. Gardiner hadn't out-and-out lied, I told her. But he hadn't spoken the truth either. He'd jumped the gun. The moment he'd said those words: *glioblastoma multiforma* and *cancer*, the harm was done.

Dr. Fountain listened. She didn't judge me. She said I was suffering from post-diagnostic stress disorder. This was common, she told me, among people diagnosed with a life-changing or life-threatening illness. The symptoms were similar to post-traumatic stress disorder, PTSD, only the trauma in question was the diagnosis. It was a relief having her give a name to my meltdown. Somehow it made me feel less crazy, less out of control. It wasn't just me. Anyone, she said, might have reacted as I had to Dr. Gardiner's bombshell. I had a "disorder," and it was treatable. She assured me this ultra-high anxiety was something I could work my way through and come out of on the other side. And I was a ready believer. I wanted to get past this, but I knew I needed help.

I had two more appointments with Dr. Fountain. She didn't say much, and she didn't need to. She gave me what I most needed—the opportunity to give voice to my fears without worrying about fallout. With Andy or my mom, I'd worry I would upset them, but not with her. She had no personal investment in me. Her interest was only professional. And I didn't want to be consoled. I didn't want to be told to snap out of it. I just wanted to be able to express myself, to be heard. I had always been pretty effective at sorting out my life once I could see clearly what was going on.

Talking to her allowed me to lay everything on the table. I was feeling angry and afraid. I tried to face up to both the fear and anger without blaming myself for feeling either. I knew the feelings would pass in their own good time without any intervention on my part because that's what emotions do: they arise and they pass through only to be replaced by another emotion. In the process, though, they devoured my energy, bloodsucking vampires that they are. So, paying attention to what I was feeling without self-judgment didn't make the pain less, but did conserve my resources. I needed every bit of strength right now to deal with this malady. The thoughts bombarding my poor brain had to be inspected with objectivity. Was the idea expressed true? False? Ambiguous? What additional information was needed to flush out the veracity of each idea? Would a list of action items help? Logical thinking helped keep me from bouncing off walls. It was one of the elephants that worked in tandem with a

My Father the Fish

relaxed body to keep the emotions from rampaging.

Psychotherapy was a strange process. Dr. Fountain didn't offer any solutions or brilliant insights and yet talking to her helped, and I was grateful. I talked a lot about my fear of making wrong decisions: Is surgery the right treatment? Maybe I should visualize an army of white blood cells blasting away at the tumor. Is Yale the right hospital? Maybe I should go to Columbia-Presbyterian. Is Dr. Piepmeier the right surgeon or should I have stuck with Dr. Vives?

"Sit with the discomfort. The fear of the unknown. Be present with it," she said. "Let facing uncertainty be one of the teachings you glean from this episode. When it all starts to feel like too much to bear, take a moment to acknowledge that and move away for a time. Come back to it only later, when you feel you can."

It was this last part of the instructions that offered some peace. I was practiced at caring for others; for self-care I was in need of instruction.

Dr. Fountain gave me room to move at my own pace. She reminded me compassion was not just for others. I needed compassion for myself as well, and she modeled for me what it might look like. I was learning to be gentler with myself at a time when my habitual pattern of harsh self-judgment was killing me. I was beating myself up for having a brain tumor and failing to deal with it unflinchingly and head on. What had I done to cause it? Was ever-present fear and anxiety the culprit? Had my messed-up mind unbalanced my energy and manifested a tumor? I was both the interrogator and the interrogated in this personal nightmare. Dr. Fountain's words were permission to not be perfect, to not get it right, now or maybe ever. She didn't tell me to relax or even suggest relaxation techniques. She didn't attempt to speak to my thinking mind and lead it step by step to a rational conclusion. She never said, "Let go." She told me to sit with the uncertainty. Observe it. Be gentle.

When I accepted Gurudev as my teacher, he asked me to

read and sign a short document in which I agreed to leave all judgment behind. This declaration was not a forgoing of discernment and discrimination. Far from it. It was a statement of the necessity to take a piercing look at my actions, thoughts, and emotions and to do so dispassionately, without praise or criticism, to simply look and see what was. But this kind of looking wasn't so simple, and it required one more ingredient—compassion for myself. Without it, it was nearly impossible to face up to all the dysfunction and ugliness that was part and parcel of every human persona.

"Observe all of it," Gurudev had said. "And know that you are not it, for you are the Self, God within."

In the aftershock of diagnosis, I had forgotten his words, and as a result the Watcher had taken her eye off the stage, leaving the many selves of Lorri to wreak their own kind of internal havoc. Dr. Fountain pointed the way back to my practice of uncritical self-observation, and I again remembered that the God I encountered in the MRI was compassion itself. If that God could embrace even the most miserable of my many selves, who was I to judge them without mercy?

Six

Barred from driving and therefore housebound, I had an abundance of time to rehash and second-guess all the doctors had told me. Facts flopped around in my head—fish too slippery to hold. During the first couple of weeks after diagnosis there were many times that I lost my way, retreating into confusion, unable to follow the breadcrumbs marking the trail to the operating room.

"Andy," I said for the umpteenth time, "if it's benign, why do I have to have surgery? Why can't we just leave it alone?"

"The tumor is pressing on your brain," he'd remind me. "You're having seizures. They'll only get worse if you don't get it out."

The facts were clear, and I was not stupid, but I was confused by the cacophony of voices clamoring inside my head.

Gurudev was a pioneer in holistic health. He practiced acupuncture and Chinese herbal medicine. Mataji was a master practitioner of amma, a therapeutic massage she had developed into a broad system of healing, after apprenticing in her native Korea with her grandmother, a traditional healer. It was rare that either of them recommended western style medical treatment—prescription drugs, surgery, chemotherapy—to their patients. I worried that to have surgery was tantamount to an act of treason: the abandonment of the principles of holistic health my teacher espoused and I had subscribed to for the past thirty years. I didn't want to be a disappointment to Gurudev, and I was ashamed of my spinelessness. If I had any real moxie, I thought, I'd say no to all the doctors and heal myself. I would visualize the tumor out of existence.

Both Gurudev and Mataji were always reasonable when it came to choosing the appropriate treatment modality. They followed an integrative approach. Gurudev objected to the term "alternative" medicine, preferring the descriptor "complementary," as the many modalities served to complete each other in a truly holistic game plan. He once sent me to see a medical doctor for an antibiotic after a stubborn sinus infection failed to respond to acupuncture and to an ophthalmologist to diagnose an eye problem. Mataji had seconded my gynecologist's recommendation I have surgery to remove a cyst that was at risk of rupturing. This feeling they would be disappointed in me had nothing to do with them. It was all me—just another hair shirt I had dropped unceremoniously over my bare shoulders.

As if that weren't painful enough, another part of me believed the brain tumor was a direct result of my failure over many years to uncritically observe my fear and anger as experiences and not as definers of who I am. Like mice who play while the cat's away, unwatched emotions disrupt the energetic balance that supports good health. By failing to observe myself, I created the very conditions in which a tumor could grow. The part of me that held myself culpable believed there was only one fitting punishment for such negligence: refuse the surgery and suffer the consequences. Shame, self-hate, and guilt tormented me, but when my effort to think prodded the Watcher to wake from its nap, my perspective changed. I found compassion for my less than perfect self, for my humanness. I allowed the feelings—all the feelings—without judgment and without indulgence. I was committed to a process of transformation. Flagellation, punishment, and absolution had no place in that pursuit.

Why *did* I have a brain tumor? I wouldn't deny the mind-body connection. Perhaps my stress and excessive emotionality had resulted in energetic imbalances and the manifestation of a tumor. Perhaps not. It really didn't matter. There was a tumor, and I had to deal with it like anything else that crossed my path—as consciously as I could.

My emotions were like runaway horses taking me on a wild ride. I only needed to wake up and grab hold of the reins to subdue them. Fear was the wildest horse of all and sometimes it got the better of me. It wasn't facing the fear, but a misguided attempt to outrun it that had me glued to my MacBook. I read up on everything I could google on meningioma, treatment options, and hospital ratings. The sheer volume of information only one click away sent me into overload. My friend Marion, an accountant, suggested I get gamma-knife radiation treatments instead of conventional surgery. She said it was safer (and who would know better than a CPA?), so I googled gamma knife. The description from the Mayo Clinic made it sound great, so clean and precise:

"In gamma-knife radiosurgery, specialized equipment focuses as many as 200 tiny beams of radiation on a tumor or other target…The precision of gamma-knife radio surgery results in minimal damage to healthy tissues surrounding the target and, in some cases, a lower risk of side effects compared with other types of radiation therapy. Also, gamma-knife radiosurgery is often a safer option than is traditional brain surgery."

How could it not be safer than sawing through my skull and poking around in my brain? Dr. Piepmeier had said the tumor was too large for gamma knife. But was that really true? Did he even do gamma knife? Maybe not. He was a surgeon, and surgeons recommend surgery. That was what they knew and it was what they got paid for. The notion that money might be a motivating factor in the recommendation for surgery sent me into a tailspin. Dr. Piepmeier had been straight-talking and caring, but that meant nothing to me in the moment. Nor did the words of four others praising his skill.

Andy had spoken to his aikido buddy, Eric, about my

diagnosis. Eric knew about meningioma. Andy was surprised. Neither he nor I had ever even heard the term before it trampled our bed of roses, but Eric's niece had had meningioma surgery last year. She swore by her surgeon.

"You'd think he walked on water," Eric had said. "His name is Dr. Piepmeier."

After his talk with Eric, Andy remembered that Jim, a fellow member of our town's Clean Energy Task Force, was a neurosurgeon. Andy gave him a call. Jim also recommended Dr. Piepmeier, "He's the top dog. World renowned."

One could imagine after three recommendations from a nurse, a former patient, and another neurosurgeon, I would have been able to relax and go with Dr. Piepmeier. But, no. I was still struggling with what to do. Though the recommendations I had received may have been signs, they weren't dynamic enough. I needed a billboard, with flashing neon lights.

And I got one.

Matt sold home entertainment systems. The same day as my diagnosis he received an email from a man requesting a price quote. The man, an MD, had a New Haven address. When Matt responded he added a postscript asking the doctor if he could recommend a neurosurgeon in New Haven for his sister who had been diagnosed with a meningioma. The doctor's reply arrived the next day: "Contact Dr. Josef Piepmeier. He's the best there is." His message was signed Dr. Vives, Neurology Staff, Yale New Haven Hospital.

What were the chances of that? Still, I kept doubting and second-guessing my decision. Face the uncertainty. Sit with the fear, Dr. Fountain had said. I did. Then, I didn't. I struggled to let go, over and over.

When I wasn't trawling the World Wide Web, I was reacting to emails from well-meaning friends who wanted to inform me of the type of treatment their Aunt Sadie had had, or the fabulous reputation of the hospital in their hometown. The more information dished out on my plate, the more anxious I became. The telephone's ring or the little "you've got mail" bing was enough to increase my heart rate and dampen my forehead and palms.

Then there was Meningioma Mommas, an online support group for women afflicted with this particular type of brain tumor. There I could immerse myself in the trials and travails of women whose prognoses were far less optimistic than mine as well as the occasional happy-ending story. One woman, two years postsurgery, was still prone to seizures and she was taking Keppra, the very same drug I was on. I had not yet considered that I might be on long-term medication, and the possibility sent me spiraling into depression. The more I read and heard, the more hysterical I became; I was like an addict, returning to the well again and again even though the water was poisoning me.

"Enough with the computer!" Andy said. "You're driving yourself crazy. You don't need any more information."

In a moment of sanity, I listened to him and shut down my web searches for good.

◆◆◆

Be sly, I thought. *I need an ally*. I was no longer seeing Dr. Fountain. She had served her purpose. I had needed to express my fear and anger toward Dr. Gardiner and she'd let me do that without passing judgment on me. By reminding me to embrace my own discomfort with compassion, she had helped to restore me to equilibrium so I could move forward. And I was, one baby step at a time. But now, I needed a different kind of ally. I needed someone with medical training, someone impartial, with no vested interest in the treatment I received, or emotional involvement with me. I knew just the person. I called her office and made an appointment to speak with Dr. Veronica Marer, my primary care doctor. Though I had only seen her a handful of times during the eight years I had been living in Woodbridge, I knew she would take the time to answer my many questions. Over the years, with only a couple of exceptions, I had showed up at her office always as a last resort after acupuncture or herbal medicine had failed to resolve the problem. A small woman with frizzy white hair and funky earrings, she wore Birkenstocks with her lab coat. When I'd gone to her for treatment of a nasty infection, she had listened, reassured, and tended to my wound daily for a week. If she thought me foolish for first having treated the problem with hot compresses and poultices of sticky, wet green clay she never let on. I always felt I had her full attention for as long as I needed it. She never commented on my preference for non-Western treatment modalities, and that was fine with me. I was tired of defending my choices before white-coated physicians.

Other doctors I had consulted over the years—gynecologists, dermatologists, orthopedists—had made no effort to mask their disdain when I questioned their approach or indicated what home remedy I had used before seeking treatment from them. This drove me crazy. How an intelligent person could dismiss out of hand something they knew absolutely nothing about was beyond me. Once, when I told a doctor my condition had improved since I had been taking a particular herbal remedy, he told me the improvement was either a coincidence or due to a placebo effect. Oh, so you've studied herbal medicine? I asked. No, he admitted. He knew nothing at all about herbs except that they didn't work. I was grateful for Dr. Marer's silence on the subject.

Dr. Marer was, as I had expected her to be, a solid pier where I could tie up my rocking boat. We sat in her cubbyhole of an office while she listened to my concerns and walked with me through each of the crazy corn mazes I had constructed and then gotten lost in. She assured me all my present symptoms—exhaustion, shakiness, ear ringing—were normal under the circumstances and due to either the brain swelling, the medication, or anxiety. After surgery, she said, any long-term medication would be adjusted to minimize side effects. This came as a great relief. She went over the meaning of my test results with me, and she explained in her own words why surgery had been recommended over any other form of treatment.

"Doing nothing is not an option here. You're having seizures. You can't *wait and see*. The tumor has to come out," she said.

Her words echoed Dr. Peipmeir's but they carried the weight of an impartial and qualified assessor. So, I moved on to my quandary over which would be the best surgeon and hospital for me. It had come to my attention my insurance would cover the surgery if I chose an out-of-state hospital. This new tidbit of information, rather than providing the comfort of expanded choices, had set off ripples of uncertainty. US News and World Report ranked the Yale New Haven neurosurgery department 32nd in the country, a ranking I found far from reassuring. Debbie, speaking as an insider, told me straight out that Mass General was the best place in the country for this surgery. My neighbor, daughter of a cancer survivor, cast her vote for Columbia-Presbyterian. My husband was wary of Yale New Haven because it was a teaching hospital, while his friend, a doctor I respected, felt I would have better care there for the same reason.

Dr. Marer sat back in her chair. She sighed, and then she smiled.

"Lorri, I have full confidence in Dr. Piepmeier and Yale New Haven. I don't think you could do better," she said with a relaxed smile. "If you still want another opinion I can refer you to a neurologist who is very conservative when it comes to surgery. But, I would be very surprised if he suggested anything different in your case."

"No," I said. "A whole team of neurologists at Yale already saw the scans. It's enough. I get it. I need the surgery."

Dr. Marer didn't respond, and we sat there together in silence for what felt like a long time. She was not running anywhere.

"There's something so familiar about all this," she said at last. "As though we've discussed it all before."

But of course, we hadn't. The brain tumor was new. A surprise from hell. She picked up my file and leafed through it.

"Ahhh, here it is. Last June. You came in for a physical, on the advice of a Kabbalist, you said. Listen, this is what you told me."

Dr. Marer read me her notes from that June visit when I had given her a detailed account of my strange meeting with Shmuel, a mystic and a practitioner of the Kabbalah, an esoteric philosophical system that forms the basis of Jewish theology. Shmuel was born in Israel and traced his roots back through a long line of Iraqi holy men. People sought his guidance on relationships, livelihood, and spiritual pursuits. His insights were derived from the pages of the Zohar, an ancient esoteric Jewish text he employed in his "readings." Many people, and I would guess most doctors, would have dismissed as nonsense the things I went on to tell her about my meeting with him. But she had bothered to set it all down in my medical file. I was impressed. She already had my trust and admiration, with this she earned my deepest respect as well.

Dr. Marer finished reading the notes in my file and set it on her desk. "Interesting, no?" she said, and we were both quiet.

◆ ◆ ◆

I had met Shmuel by chance, six months earlier. The congregation of a Sephardic synagogue in Brooklyn had sponsored his visit to the States because they were in need of

My Father the Fish

his counsel. On his way to Brooklyn he made a stopover in Connecticut to visit a mutual friend of ours. That friend had asked if Shmuel could stay with Andy and me over Shabbat, because he himself did not live within walking distance to the synagogue. We had agreed to the arrangement. After getting to know Shmuel a little over dinner, and with the assurance of our friend that Shmuel was the real deal—learned, intuitive and gifted with insight—I made arrangements to sit with him for a reading the following week. I longed for a blast of insight from someone with farther reaching vision than I had. I thought it was what I needed to disperse the fog that had settled over my rocky road to enlightenment. This looking outside myself for answers, unable to believe that I already had everything I needed, was my long-standing, misguided pattern.

At the appointed time, I found Shmuel seated at a cherry wood conference table in a medium-sized office at the Jewish Community Center. He was fortyish with an untamed beard and dark restless eyes. Empty Pepsi cans and heavy leather-bound books lay scattered in front of him. He offered no greeting. I waited, then sat down across from him at the table. I was uncomfortable with the silence, but I didn't know how to begin. I thought maybe I should start with a question. Before I could form one, Shmuel asked me for my Hebrew name and birth date.

His readings relied upon gematria, an ancient numerological system. Without pencil and paper he computed the numerical value of my name and birthday by adding up the values assigned to the constituent letters. Arriving at a sum, he picked through the books in front of him and selected a volume of the Zohar. Without hesitation, he turned to a specific page and counted down the lines. I was prickling with excitement, anticipating holy words and illuminated discourse. But he began with medical advice. "Get a blood analysis," he said.

"Why?" I asked. I felt fine.

"Something not right," he said in heavily accented English. "Immune system all wrong, hormones too low. Tell doctor to test you."

Test me for what? As though he had heard my thoughts, Shmuel responded that the doctor would know. I should just go. He spoke with an urgency that caused cold sweat to bead up on my skin and reignited an old apprehension of a future cut short by a fatal illness. This fear was not something I had ever given voice to—in case the words themselves could coax the disease into being—but now Shmuel had voiced it for me.

I was relieved when he moved on to pronouncements of my strengths, "a good, kind person," and my weaknesses, "too trusting, failure to recognize some people are evil." He said my work with the aged would further my spiritual growth, and I had healing power in my hands I should develop. *This is good*, I thought. *This is what I came for. Stuff I can use.*

Then, Shmuel went silent. He staggered out of his chair and darted from the room. I was stunned. *What was that about?* Five minutes later he returned. His button-down shirt, a dingy white, was stuffed sloppily into his black trousers. He was red-eyed and sweating. He spoke to me in rapid-fire Hebrew, and I missed most of what he said. But his agitation and repetition of the word *hara*—evil—caused the hair on my arms to stand at attention. Finally, he slowed down enough and resumed in broken English.

"Had to run from room. Bad energy from your head, make me sick."

Bad energy? My heart pummeled the inside of my chest. I remembered an incident from thirty years earlier.

During the time I lived in the ashram, I had been managing the small health food store we operated in the basement of the Wholistic Health Center. A man came in after his acupuncture treatment to purchase herbs and vitamins. I was helping him locate the items on his list when my head started to spin, and I felt overcome by nausea. I ran from the store. Later on I learned from one of the acupuncturists that this man had stage four cancer. He was dying. I had, I supposed, picked up on the grossly imbalanced energy of his diseased body.

Was that what Shmuel was feeling now? I followed him with my eyes. He was pacing. When he stopped, he settled into his chair. "What you have to do with Indians?" he asked.

"Nothing," I said. "What kind of Indians... from India?"

"No. American Indians."

I shrugged.

"There's sign above your head. Indian symbol. It block you."

Shmuel crossed his arms over his chest, his dark eyes boring into me. I waited, hoping for some further explanation. *Symbol of what? Blocking me how?*

"Someone want you dead. Someone very evil. They put curse on you."

A curse? This is crazy, I thought, and yet again I began to sweat.

Shmuel rummaged through his battered briefcase, pulled out a small fat book, and began rifling through the pages. "Here," he said, pointing to the Hebrew text. "This prayer. Repeat for protection. Every day. Then curse will be lifted."

He handed me the book and without so much as a goodbye, shalom, or *le'hitraoat,* left the room. This time he did not return.

I was not sure what to make of Shmuel's words. I took seriously his insistence I go for medical tests, but the business about signs and symbols pushed my rational, practical self to its limits. Although I tried to dismiss his warning as nonsense, it nagged at me without relent. And so, hedging my bets, I invoked the incantation. Every day. In Hebrew. For weeks. The prayer ran on for ten pages. "May it be your will O Lord, my God, and God of my Fathers, that you will protect me from all evil..." I also went to Dr. Marer for a physical.

The words of the prayer wove a misty veil that seemed to conceal and shelter me, and the physical turned up no sign of illness. But it was mid-summer before I decided I'd done enough. I repressed the lingering feelings of foreboding and found a home for the prayer book on my bookshelf. I got busy with the garden. I finished up my master's degree and grew excited about launching the sage-ing programs. I did not want to be sick. I could not contemplate dying.

That summer I had ignored all the little signs something was not right. Instead I had made excuses: menopause, mindlessness, too much meditation. I had dismissed the signs and discounted Shmuel's warning. Yet, he had known. In his own way, he had seen the tumor. Modern medicine relied upon imaging: X-ray, CAT scan, MRI, ultrasound, thermography. Each technology produced a different image: sharp or fuzzy, black and white, or Technicolor. The image, no matter what produced it, required interpretation by a radiologist. This specialist with medical training could read "tumor" or "fracture" or "torn ligament" from the film. Shmuel saw another kind of image, one that also required special interpretive skills: those of a mystic. He saw a symbol hovering above my head and sensed a negative energy field around it, which he interpreted as a threat to my health. *Was he wrong?*

Shmuel had given me a sign, but I wasn't paying attention, not fully, anyway. I suspected there were always signs, but I didn't always have the eyes to see or the ears to hear. So often an unexpected person crossed my path and delivered exactly the words I needed, or a door suddenly opened to reveal new possibilities, or a new solution suggested itself where there seemed to have been none. Maybe signs were like broadcasts of a deeper wisdom carried over the airwaves and audible only if I set my tuner to the right station. Sometimes I thought the broadcast originated within myself—not from the cast of *The Story of Lorri*, but from the Self. Other times I imagined an all-loving god, who wanted nothing other than my greatest good, broadcasting signs in my direction. Either way, my receiver had to be tuned to the right spot on the dial, and that meant I had to get out of my own way. I had to relax. I had to be open. The Watcher had to be present to keep a dispassionate eye on the action if I were going to see the signs.

I had fretted for a couple of weeks over who should do the surgery even while all fingers had been pointing to Dr. Piepmeier. *Weren't these signs of a sort?* Only after my visit with Dr. Marer was I able to put the question of which surgeon to use to rest. Dr. Piepmeier would put the saw to my skull, and he'd do it at the hospital closest to my home. My next appointment with him was short, cordial, business-like. He was satisfied I was now in my right mind and allowed me to sign the consent forms. I had hoped to leave his office with a date for the surgery, but that was not to be. His surgical assistant called me later that week to let me know the surgery was scheduled for February 12, another four weeks away. It would be a long wait, and the doubt surfaced again and again, each time taking my breath away and dragging me under in a sandy whirl of confusion and fear. The doubt came. It went. I didn't have to cling to it. I could watch, bear the discomfort, and let it fly by in its own time, which it always did.

It also helped to replace the doubt with facts. I prepared a crib sheet I took to carrying around in my pocket for ready reference. It read like this:

The Facts
1. The tumor is technically a cancer, but it's classified BENIGN.
2. It's causing seizures and swelling in my brain.
3. Because of its size and location, surgery is the best and safest option.
4. Radiation treatments could damage the brain.

5. Leaving it alone is not an option; the seizures will continue and the swelling is dangerous.
   6. It is slow growing, so surgery isn't urgent.

The very act of reading and taking in the facts on my six-point list helped to pull me out of the muck. Rallying the facts also called up the Watcher in me, and once she was present everything else got easier. It would then be apparent to me I was not *suffering* from a brain tumor. I was *suffering* from my investment in the random and false thoughts associated with the brain tumor and its treatment. I had had but one encounter with one physician who had raised the possibility of an aggressive brain cancer. That possible diagnosis had been debunked 24 hours later, yet since that time I had relived the terror of that moment again and again. I was at the mercy of only one thing: the words I kept repeating in my head. Each time I saw the truth of that, I experienced peace. It was a tenuous peace, like moving into the eye of the hurricane, but I was already making progress toward regaining my equilibrium. I had a practice to fall back on. I was not without tools. I didn't need to find anything new, I had only to return.

Seven

Andy's older brother, David, is a family therapist. In his practice he uses a system of psychotherapy known as Healing From the Body Level Up (HBLU). This system is an integration of biomedical science, psychology, applied kinesiology, neurolinguistic programming, and other energy-based healing systems. I was familiar with his methods. Six months earlier, after my encounter with Shmuel and his pronouncement of the curse hanging over my head, David had worked with me using the HBLU system. He, more so than I, took the curse very seriously and thought we should address it, and I was willing to go along. The results were surprising.

David had asked me to close my eyes, relax, and visualize the Indian symbol Shmuel had identified as the agent of the curse. I pictured a heavy cast iron shield hovering about a foot above my head.

"From your soul and deepest wisdom," David said. "What do you need to break the shield and remove the curse?"

"I need God's help," I said without hesitation and to my own surprise. When had I last asked God for help?

David told me to imagine energy rising upwards from my belly, traveling to my chest, and out the top of my head. I closed my eyes and put my attention on my belly and pictured a fiery ball of energy. With my mind I coaxed the energy upwards. It felt hot as it traveled through my torso into my neck and finally burst out the top of my skull and shattered the shield. *Had there been a curse? Was it now broken?* I didn't know what to think, but I did know what I had just experienced.

David asked, "From your soul and deepest wisdom, is there anything else you need?"

"I need to forgive God," I said, surprising myself again. Where was this God stuff coming from? The All-Knowing-Ever-Presence that figured into my personal theology was not one to blame or not blame. It didn't cause good things or bad things to happen to me. It didn't even notice me.

Whatever did I have to forgive God for? I sat with the question in silence. The answer took shape like a phantom arising out of the darkness: after almost forty years, a teenager still grieved in me, and she blamed God for taking Marcia away. As soon as the notion coalesced, I knew in my gut it was the truth. I was angry at God. I also knew I was ready to be free of this pain. Reb Zalman once introduced a talk on forgiveness by saying, "Not forgiving someone is like stabbing yourself in the stomach to hurt the person standing behind you." Without need for further thought or analysis, I withdrew my knife and laid it on the table. In a rush of tears I forgave the God that back then, I had never considered relating to.

That whole HBLU experience with David had been very strange, yet I felt so much better afterwards. Whether it was relief that the curse (*was there such a thing?*) was broken or the relief of making peace with a God I didn't know I'd been angry with, I couldn't be sure. But better was better, so when David drove down from Boston to work his magic again, I agreed to give the HBLU another go. We left Andy in the living room and retreated to the bedroom for some privacy. Our work together did not have the same mysterious quality as the first time, though I did feel calmer and more self-contained afterward. When David asked me if there was anything else I needed, I brought Andy, not God, into the mix.

"I need Andy to listen to me. Really hear me. I need his

support." I said.

I knew Andy loved me. He would go to the end of the world for me, but he was often unable to hear me. Really hear me. We all see the world through our own lens, and he was no exception. When I spoke, what he perceived and responded to was often very different from what I was intending, asking, needing. This drove me crazy. More than that, it hurt me. I accused him of seeing only what he wanted to see and hearing only what he wanted to hear. No matter how well intended, the more he asserted his point of view, the more disregarded and invisible I felt. I needed him to be there for me. I couldn't go through this alone and I hadn't the energy to argue with him, endlessly re-explaining myself. If I said I was tired and wanted to lay down and rest, he was apt to push me to take an invigorating walk. I didn't want to have to debate the matter with him. When I had mentioned to him a neighbor was going to come visit the next afternoon, he told me I should invite her for lunch. I was outraged. "Don't you get it yet?" I had screamed in his face. "I have no energy. It's an effort to make my own lunch. You want me to entertain guests now too!" He had stared at me blankly. He didn't get it.

I asked David to talk to him. I hoped my sharing this personal relationship issue with David would demonstrate to Andy how desperate I was for him to hear me. I never asked him if David had talked to him, but his behavior during my recovery suggested that he had.

Unconditional love has been defined as the willingness to go to hell so your beloved could go to heaven. I knew it was hard for Andy to let go of his world view to try and see through my eyes, but he made the effort. In the coming months, Andy was there for me, hearing me, and giving me what I needed more often than not.

On a Saturday evening soon after David's visit, Andy stood at the kitchen sink cleaning up the dinner dishes while I sat curled on the recliner huddled under an afghan, a comforting, if inadequate, shield against a world that loomed dangerous and unpredictable. Tova, our shaggy, black, long haired mutt, was asleep on my lap. The warmth and weight of her body and regular rhythm of her breath at another time would have soothed me, but memories of Moshe were haunting me.

He had lived in the house above our apartment in Israel eight years earlier. Like me, he had a benign brain tumor and, like mine, his had to come out.

"Such a sad story," a neighbor had said. "They told him everything would be fine. But it wasn't fine. A slip of the knife and he wound up a vegetable."

Moshe could not speak. He could not hold his head up. He drooled. I had caught only glimpses of him slumped in his wheelchair, but during the year we lived below him, his frustrated grunts and howls had seeped down between our ceiling tiles.

When I brought up Moshe to Andy, he tried to reassure me. "You're not Moshe," he would say. Then he would cite Dr. Piepmeier's impeccable credentials and remind me of all the recommendations that had come with such uncanny serendipity. Still, I was not comforted. Moshe, too, had had a skilled surgeon.

I heard a knock at the front door. Andy turned off the kitchen faucet. There were footsteps and then voices. Two couples followed Andy into the living room—our friends, Igor and Nina, and a man and woman I did not know. The visit was unexpected and I wasn't feeling very social. I pulled the afghan tighter around me and offered a weak smile and a nod in response to the introductions.

"We're here to pray for you," Igor said. "Prayer is powerful. And it's proven."

Igor is a physicist with the soul of a mystic. Once, with a seriousness bordering on reverence, he confided in me, "Everything is energy." My guess was that on this night, he intended to harness some of it for my benefit. Even after my own episode of spontaneous prayer during the MRI, I remained uncomfortable with the very premise of prayer, conjuring for me, as it still did, the image of a Big Daddy in the sky listening attentively to my every word. Yet when Igor dragged an ottoman to the center of the living room and instructed me to sit, I did so.

    He and his prayer posse gathered in a circle around me and, chanting my Hebrew name *Rivka bat Batsheva*, they lifted their arms above their heads and then down again. Up and down, up and down, as though I were the fire and they the fanners of the flame. Under ordinary circumstances I would have squirmed. Circles and chanting and waving of hands lay far outside my comfort zone. But there was nothing ordinary about a brain tumor, and I hadn't the energy to wall them out. Just as I had let David do his HBLU woo-woo, I closed my eyes and opened my heart to let in their healing intention.

    My breath entrained to the rhythm of their chant, and with each wave of their hands and repetition of my name a vibratory pulsation flowed from them into me. It was beyond comforting. It produced a feeling of well-being that was not dependent upon the health of my body—a peace that was not contingent upon anything at all.

    Over the weeks to come many people told me they would pray for me, and I was grateful. I had read studies showing sick people who were prayed for fared better than those who weren't. This proved true even when the patient had no idea he was being prayed for and when those offering prayers were strangers to the patient. But I didn't need science to confirm what I had experienced for myself. I felt something palpable when I was in the center of the prayer circle, like the vibration of a booming bass line.

    Andy was always praying for people he didn't know. He received a rabbi's weekly email with a list of names of people who were ill. He prayed for them and he added my name to the rabbi's list, so strangers began praying for me too. Some of my friends were praying as well—Sarah and her Jewish Women's Prayer Circle, my friend Rosalie—a Catholic who put great store in the power of prayer—and others. The more people who found out what was going on with me, the more people were saying "I'll pray for you," and I found myself simply answering "thank you" and meaning it.

That evening Igor left me a copy of *Healing Visualizations: Creating Health Through Imagery* by Gerald Epstein MD. Though I had no hope a brain tumor could be imagined out of existence—at least not by an unskillful meditater like me—I was willing to give visualization a try. I was sure it couldn't hurt and left room for the possibility that it could indeed help. The images suggested in the book made me feel self-conscious. I didn't think I could work with them, so I decided to come up with images of my own.

After breakfast the next morning, I got right back into bed. Sitting cross-legged, propped up against pillows with the covers across my lap, I closed my eyes and brought my attention to my breath. I was ready to visualize healing images, but I didn't know where to start, so I listened to the sound of the air drawing in and rushing out like a wave racing up the shore and then retreating. Soon, pictures began to form in my mind and I retreated deeper and deeper within…

I recognize the place. It is the beach at Keawakapu not far from where I once lived in Hawaii on the slopes of Haleakela. At low tide seawater settles into depressions in the massive slabs of rock, lingering remnants of past eruptions that sent lava flowing into the Pacific. These pools are rich with life—small fish, turquoise and sunflower yellow, deep purple anemones, midnight blue mollusks, and orange-veined shrimp.

I am floating in a tidal pool lulled by the gentle roll of the waves and the rhythm of my breath. The sun has warmed the pool, but cooler water cascades over me and lifts me onto a raft of shimmering bubbles that drifts out into open sea, westward toward the island of Lanai. The current carries the raft and me to a rocky prominence emerging from the sea. It is my skull, and there is an opening at its base like the mouth of a cave. The ocean rushes in pushing the raft along. Water flows all around me. It is living water, healing water.

The raft glides into the chamber that houses my brain. The tumor protrudes. It is a spongy growth on the parietal lobe. Paddling with my hands and gently kicking my feet I cause the waters to trickle over my brain and caress the tumor. I feel no anger, no fear, only peace.

Soon the images dissolved, but reveling in the peace they brought I lingered a bit, eyes still closed. Then with slow even breaths I opened my eyes and came fully back into my bedroom. My mind drifted like an untethered boat in a calm sea, and a question arose from the depths of me. *The tumor is not expected to kill me, so why is it here?* Like Andy, I believed in a Grand Design. If I had a brain tumor, there was a reason for it. A Jewish prayer goes "God, please restore me to health so my instrument can do Your Will most perfectly." It occurred to me then that, perhaps, to accomplish what I was meant to accomplish in this life, a perfect instrument was not the best instrument. The tumor had already compromised my balance and my ability to orient in space. I had been forewarned these deficits might turn out to be permanent, but what if these apparent disabilities provided me with exactly the conditions I needed to grow spiritually, to become someone who *would* do God's Will? The tumor was here to be my teacher, I was sure of that. The lessons would unfold over time. It was up to me to be vigilant and watch for them. For the first time since my diagnosis, I was unafraid. I did not feel threatened by the tumor. I felt almost tender toward it.

On the days that followed, I set aside time in the early morning to close my eyes, relax and let my mind carry me out to sea, intentionally revisiting the story that had first unfolded of its own accord. Each day I visualized the same scenes, like attending repeat performances of a well-loved play. On the sixth day, however, the raft transformed into a fish with long cat whiskers and iridescent scales that sparkled in the sunlight. I had not written this new scene into the script. It was not under my direction. The fish had conjured itself and the story took a new turn.

I am comfortable on the back of this fish that travels me to the sea cave that is my skull. The salty water rushes in, and the fish and I are pushed into a chamber where the tumor sits, a wise elder upon a throne. We circle. The fish flicks its tail, again and again, sending the living water cascading over the tumor—a balm to my swollen brain.

The fish slows, and I slide off its back and address the tumor.

"I know it was never your intention to harm me," I say. "But you have. So, when Dr. Piepmeier comes for you with his scalpel release yourself into his hands and go. Leave me with your teaching, but leave none of your cells behind."

I turn, and for the first time fish and I are face to face. I look into its eyes. They are my father's eyes. The white whiskers on the flattened fish face are my father's handlebar mustache. He has come to carry me on his back again as he had when I was a small child. The comfort I feel is deep and velvety.

We approach the shore. I slip off my father's back. His eyes are glistening, and he blinks at me before swimming off.

I don't want to lose you again, I thought, as his image grew hazy. During the last three months of my dad's life, I had spent many afternoons smoothing Vaseline on his lips, monitoring his care, and being present for him. I talked to him about living and dying. I listened to his sputtered words and witnessed the upturn of his lip and the plea in his eye. He breathed his last breath with me by his side, his eyes staring unblinking, awestruck and shining. He was in the place he most wanted to be—his home. Our connection was a strong one, and in the weeks remaining before my surgery I returned each day to ride the waves out to the sea cave upon the back of my father the fish. I never spoke to the fish as he carried me out to sea and to shore again. I didn't need to. I knew in my heart my father had come to do for me what, in the end, I had done for him. He came to be by my side as I walked this hard road.

◆◆◆

An aphorism: *One must take the hardships of life and render them spiritual.* I had thought of these words often over the years. They had the power to free me from the saddlebags of self-pity I slung over my back. They didn't advocate fantasy by suggesting hardships were anything other than hardships, rather, they spelled out the kind of change in perception required to shift from an attitude of "woe is me, I've got the weight of the world on my shoulders," to one of "I welcome the opportunities to grow that await me".

I wasn't Pollyanna. This wasn't about turning lemons into lemonade. No amount of sugar was going to improve the taste of this tumor. It had already brought my career aspirations to a halt, and who knew what else the aftermath of surgery would bring? Yet, I was galvanized and enthusiastic about meeting whatever would come head on. I had facilitated a shift in perception by thinking of the journey through tumor treatment and recovery as my teacher and not my personal tragedy. I worked hard to remember that death was not an abstraction but a reality that one day would be mine to experience firsthand. The philosopher, Dr. Paul Brunton, said an inner detachment is possible when people come to see that the very existence of their possessions, properties, and persons are not secure, but can be snatched away in a moment. "…sorrow leads to understanding," he said. "Every tear becomes a tutor."

Embracing death went hand in hand with remembering who I am, and am not. I have a body—one I must feed and care for and keep healthy— but I, the unchanging Self, am not this body. Staying ever present with this truth was no small thing. When the ringing in my ear reached a decibel level that could well evacuate an entire building, and fatigue threatened to pull me under like a pair of cement shoes, it was easy to become consumed by the experience. But remembering was the only way out. It effected a radical change in perspective and opened the door to a new way of seeing and being in the world.

I took to singing a chant that had been part of the soundtrack of my ashram days. I sang it now, over and over again. I sang loud, I sang strong, and the words resonated with the Self.

> Bliss and knowledge,
> Bliss and knowledge.
> Bliss, bliss, absolute.
> I am bliss and knowledge.
> Bliss, bliss, absolute.
>
> Not this body.
> Not this mind.
> Not these emotions am I.
> I am bliss and knowledge.
> Bliss, bliss absolute.

When it came right down to it, what I wanted most was to be happy. Not broad-smile-bouncy-gait-happy, but the happy born of a quiet peace. And I knew that was possible. I had tasted it before. But it was all too easy to forget that the road to that kind of happy stretched out in only one direction, and the direction was *in*. Gurudev had often said, "If you want to get from NY to LA, hopping an eastbound train isn't going to get you there." With the assist of the high voltage shock delivered by the brain tumor diagnosis, this was the teaching I remembered now: the unequivocal necessity of knowing the direction in which to travel in order to reach my destination.

"Man is born to live, to suffer, and to die, and what

befalls him is a tragic lot. There is no denying this in the final end. But we must deny it all along the way," wrote Thomas Wolfe. From my perspective, he got the diagnosis right but prescription wrong. Suffering *was* fundamental to life, but we *mustn't* deny it all along the way. There was no way out if the truth was trampled under. Life was always going to be dumping on my doorstep, and when it didn't I could still be depended upon to feel depressed, angry, unfairly treated, or afraid about something from time to time. The peace I am after is attainable only because it is dependent solely upon the way I choose to see the world and not on what the world is offering up in the moment.

After a few weeks, tired of sitting home alone, I went into work with Andy. He set me up with my laptop in an empty office and I busied myself. By afternoon I was exhausted. By the time Andy was ready to leave for home, I was weak with fatigue and feeling pretty miserable.

"Do you want to go out for dinner?" Andy said.

There was nothing prepared at home, but I hadn't the energy to sit in a restaurant. I told him I would be fine with a bowl of cereal and closed my eyes for the rest of the ride, wishing though, for something more substantial than Cheerios.

Walking up our front path in the early evening darkness I could just make out a bulky shape on the bench by our kitchen door. It was a shopping bag filled to the brim with containers and foil wrapped trays. Nina, from the prayer posse, had dropped off a whole dinner—Russian borscht, butternut squash turnovers and apple cobbler.

This I thought, already salivating, *is like a Christmas miracle.* Grateful didn't even come close to describing what I was feeling.

I knew a good number of people from my Sage-ing Guild and from the community—the JCC, the shul, my work. These were people with whom I had friendly but casual relationships. Yet as word got out I was awaiting surgery, so many of them came forward to offer support. I received many get well cards, some from people I didn't know—guys from Andy's dojo, friends of my mother-in-law, and a few I was never able to identify. Judith, a sage-ing teacher whom I had never warmed up to when we'd met at meetings or conferences, sent me a handmade card each week with a brief but caring note inside. Neighbors, Cheryl and Joel, came over one afternoon and offered to take a walk with me. I don't know how they knew that was just what I needed. I had been feeling cooped up. My balance was poor and I was afraid to go out on my own. We walked and I talked and they really listened. Theirs was one small yet precious act, and with it they crossed the boundary from casual acquaintance into the territory of friendship.

Help came from the most unlikely places. So many people whom I never would have expected to reach out to me did so. At the same time, there were others whom I assumed would be there for me who weren't. When a call or visit I hoped for never came, I felt sad, disappointed, and even a little hurt. Sometimes I pictured myself getting even by withdrawing from the relationship. But that's where it ended, with a picture. I didn't try to guess why some people were there for me and some weren't. I knew each of us saw through our own eyes and created our own world. In the *Tao Te Ching*, Lao Tse says, "Ever desireless one can see the mystery. Ever desiring one can see the manifestation." Releasing my requirements of others and not judging them was essential to removing the shroud from the mystery that was God. My requirements kept me earthbound and I wanted to soar free.

Eight

One afternoon in early January I made my way down a narrow shoveled path to the mailbox at the end of our driveway. It was stuffed with the usual—a circular from Stop & Shop, utility bills, the occasional get-well card—and a padded envelope from Rabbi Zalman Schachter-Shalomi. I opened it right there by the side of the road. The plain manila package, plastered with postage stamps, contained a CD in a paper sleeve. On the diskette, handwritten in black marker, were the words *For Your Healing* —*Reb Zalman*. A short typed note was tucked in the paper sleeve.

"Dear Lorri," it read. "I'm sending you a CD for your healing. I used it myself when I was in the hospital and found it helpful. I will keep you in my prayers for a complete and total recovery. Reb Zalman."

I had never considered telling him about my tumor, but Rosalie, my friend and sage-ing mentor, had. She knew I had a connection with him, and she knew he was a rebbe, someone special. What a blessing that turned out to be for me.

Clutching the CD and the rest of the mail, I retraced my footprints in the snow and retreated indoors. In my bedroom, I read Reb Zalman's note again, savoring each word. I had been delivered a treasure by parcel post, and I delayed playing it for the pure enjoyment of anticipating what was to come.

There was a soft tap-tap at the door. "Ok if I come in?" Andy said, pushing the door open a crack. "What did you get?"

"It's a CD. From Reb Zalman. He made it for me."

"Really? How cool is that. Did you listen yet?"

I hadn't. I wanted to listen to it alone. It felt sacred somehow. Sent to me for my healing, it was not a casual recording to be passed around. Andy left and closed the door behind him as I placed the disk inside my CD player and fit the earplugs in place.

"*Ana elna refah na la.*" Reb Zalman sang numerous repetitions of this verse from Numbers 12:13, Moses' prayer for the healing of his sister, Miriam. He chanted first the Hebrew, then the English. "Heal her Lord. Please heal her."

His voice, accompanied by the strumming of an autoharp, was soothing though not melodic. After several minutes of chanting, he spoke words of such love and compassion that, unable to contain them, I felt I would burst. He spoke to me. He spoke to God. His words fostered between us the intimacy of fellow travelers. He guided me in a healing visualization and through the process taught me how to speak to God and how I could use prayer to support my own healing.

"I open myself to You, God," Reb Zalman intoned, "to be known by You to be seen by You. See me from outside of me, see me from the environment, see me in my environment and see me on the inside of me. I want to be fully transparent to You, God. I open myself fully to You."

My theology allowed for God's transcendence, but here was an immanent God, being invited in. It was an invitation I had longed to extend but hadn't known how. The experience I had had chanting Gam ki eilech… in the MRI had been as powerful as a lightning strike, and I could not count on it illuminating me twice. I heard in Reb Zalman's words about transparency the key to again bringing God within reach of my fingertips. I had to open myself fully, and this meant giving up the baseless pictures I held of myself, the desires I clung to, the aversions I defended, and my requirements for how life should be. A tall order. The tallest, perhaps, but something well worth striving for if the reward was an intimate relationship with God.

My Father the Fish

In a letter I wrote to Reb Zalman after listening to the CD for many weeks, I told him he had provided me with a "conduit between my head and my heart." This was a connection I had sensed was broken, or perhaps had never been whole. Many years ago, Gurudev had encouraged me to practice meditating on the guru in the heart as a means of establishing a deeper connection to him and the teaching. I failed miserably. He had said to me, "You're not getting it. You are still in your head. You must drop the ideas into your heart." I never understood what that meant. I was so frustrated, wanting badly what I could not seem to grasp hold of. Praying along with Reb Zalman and working at becoming transparent was narrowing the gap between my head and my heart. I was coming to understand transcendence did not preclude immanence. God was one, without contradiction, and both were true.

The prayers and psalms that traditional Jews recite daily are quite lengthy and are read from a siddur. There are many versions of this prayer book, and most people are wed to the version that reflects their particular take on Jewish practice. Andy preferred to mix things up. He owns many prayer books and uses them all. He said that way the recitation didn't become mechanical. One siddur in his collection was a slim volume containing Reb Zalman's free translation of the morning prayer service. One morning after he had left for work, I noticed it lying open on the coffee table and thumbed through it. One prayer caught my attention: *Elohai nishamah shenatata bi tehora hi...*

> My God, the soul You have given me is fresh and pure. You shaped it. You formed it. You breathed it into me, and You keep me breathing. One day, You will take this soul from me, and I will have breathed my last breath in this body. And you will resuscitate me to life of the spirit. For each breath you

111

still have for me, I thank You God.

This was a recitation of gratitude that I could say from my heart. In words that were pragmatic and loving, the speaker of the prayer faced physical mortality without a whisper of fear, while acknowledging both the immortality and the source of the soul. I sequestered the little prayer book and incorporated this thank you prayer into my own evolving morning practice.

♦♦♦

Surgery was a month away. I had my life as well as my head to get in order. I was not only our chief cook and bottle washer, I was also our financial manager and bookkeeper. I typed out a list of account numbers and passwords for Andy. I made sure to stay up-to-date with bill paying, and I tackled a tall stack of papers that had been waiting patiently to be filed. If Andy needed anything, I wanted to be sure he could find it in the folder where it belonged. I called our insurance company to check on coverage, I finished up outstanding projects for my client, and I got in touch with Raizy.

Raizy was my friend Devorah's teenage daughter. I knew her pretty well from a March of the Living trip to Poland and Israel that we had gone on three years earlier to commemorate the sixtieth anniversary of the liberation of Aushwitz-Birkenau concentration camps. She was smart and funny and had a huge heart, and I needed a favor. Not long before I landed in the ER, Fred, an eighty-three-year-old student of mine from The Towers had taken a bad fall and, after a brief hospitalization, had wound up in a rehab facility. He had no family nearby and he was so hard of hearing that phone visits were all but impossible. He was very lonely and so I had been visiting him at rehab, where we would talk poetry. Fred is a poet. I had promised to bring him a notebook so he could continue writing while he recuperated.

The hard-bound journal I had purchased was sitting on my dresser.

I called Devorah to see if it would be okay if I asked Raizy to bring Fred the journal and, if she felt comfortable, to visit him as long as he was at the rehab. Devorah thought this was a great idea, and Raizy responded with enthusiasm. I was so relieved to know Fred would continue to have some company. Raizy visited Fred during those weeks I was housebound and long after as well. Even Devorah got into the act, bringing Fred delectables from her kitchen, taking him on outings, and visiting him on holidays.

With Fred and the day-to-day household concerns taken care of, I turned my attention to myself. I had work to do. Pithy adages kept coming to mind: First you must put your shoulder to the grindstone; God helps those who help themselves; without a deposit, there's no return. I knew the outcome of my surgery would be affected by my physical and emotional state going in. I was not intending to sit and wait for surgery. I was going to do whatever I could to prepare myself body and mind, and I was going to accept help.

First, the body. A floor-to-ceiling bookshelf in my den contained volume after volume on herbs, homeopathy, nutrition, and traditional Chinese medicine. I combed the shelves and pulled out an assortment of texts to consult. I read and I took notes. That evening I asked Andy to give me a ride to our public library. There I consulted an illuminating tome, *Surgery and Its Alternatives* by Sandra A. and David J. McLanahan M.D. I took more notes. By early the next day, I had a plan that included a pre-op and post-op regime.

It had long been my practice to take specific vitamins and herbs to boost my immune system and promote overall good health, but I had discontinued the herbs as soon as I was put on Keppra to prevent seizures. Herbs are quite complex. Unlike a pharmaceutical drug, based on a single active constituent, the therapeutic benefit of herbs comes from the combined effect of the many phytochemicals found in the plant. There was no way I could know for sure if any one of these active agents might interfere with the Keppra and I didn't want to take a chance. I kept up with my vitamins and minerals until two weeks before the surgery, then I eliminated the vitamin E, which can interfere with blood clotting.

Homeopathic medicines were at the heart of my plan. Traditional homeopathy has been a part of western medicine for more than two hundred years and is based on the theory that like cures like. In other words, a substance that at full strength would cause a specific disease symptom in healthy people will, in an extremely diluted form, alleviate that same symptom in sick people. This does sound counter-intuitive, but consider the function of a flu or vaccine; the rationale is much the same, although homeopathic medicines are prepared very differently than vaccines. They are often extreme dilutions. The ones I was taking were so dilute Andy referred to them as bottles of no-molecules. He was not far off. In a 30C dilution of the herb Echinacea, for example, a scientist with all the right equipment would not be able to detect a single molecule of the herb in the solution. So, yes, it is hard to believe these medicines could be effective. And yet they are. I had used them for a variety of conditions in the past with good result. Best of all, because they are so dilute, they do not cause side effects or interactions with other drugs. I felt confident they would help, but I was not going to Lone Ranger this. My plan was not to circumvent my physicians but to join the team. I sent Dr. Piepmeier an email detailing my regimen. He responded within a few hours. He was fine with it as long as Dr. Silverman, the anesthesiologist, agreed.

I went to my appointment with Dr. Silverman armed with photocopies of pertinent pages from the McLanahans' book, a scholarly article on homeopathy, and a book on the subject from my own library. I knew the chances were pretty good Dr. Silverman would know nothing on the subject and view the whole thing as voodoo. My plan was to educate him. I wasn't looking for his blessing. Yet I knew he would ask, "What are you taking?" and I was committed to full-disclosure. I wanted him to be confident nothing I was doing would interfere with whatever drug cocktail he would be injecting into me on the day of surgery. I laid out my plan:

> For 2 days before surgery take 3 pills, 4x/day: 30C Gelsemium Sempervirens or Arsenicum album to prevent anxiety; 30C Arnica Montana to prevent pain and bruising; 30C Ferrum Phosphoricum to prevent excessive bleeding and infection.
>
> Post-surgery, if needed, take 3 pills, 4x/day: 200C Arnica Montana for pain, bruising and bleeding; 200C Phosphorus if Arnica fails to control bleeding; 200C Hypericum if nerves were severed.

Dr. Silverman had heard of homeopathy, but by his own admission, had no knowledge of the science behind it. He did know the medicines were extremely dilute, and therefore, he had no qualms about my taking the pills. He considered them to be harmless and doubted their effectiveness. I could have left it at that, but his ignorance bothered me. I gave him the articles and the book hoping he would read them. I didn't expect him to embrace homeopathy as part of his practice, but I thought he was sure to have other patients ask him about taking homeopathics and this way, when they did, he'd be able to answer their questions.

Some time after our meeting I wrote to thank him:

"Your willingness to take my needs and my approach to my health care seriously was extremely important to me. I think to be a healer who heals you must have an open mind and an open heart to let in all those intangibles that contribute to healing, as well as the tangibles God also put on this Earth as healing aids, though these were not covered in your medical school education."

The more I saw of the ignorance and arrogance fostered by our medical school system, the more compelled I was to acknowledge even those very faint shining stars who could help light the way for others. Dr. Silverman had heard me out, listened with interest to my brief discourse on homeopathy, and agreed to my plan without a hint of disdain.

I wanted to be in tip-top shape before the surgery. I knew exercise was important, but the damn Keppra had me feeling so fatigued I could do little more than practice tai chi and take walks in my neighborhood when weather permitted. When the series of movements that make up the tai chi form are executed with focused attention, relaxation, and precision, it is a moving meditation. The shift of weight, the lifting of a leg, the sweep of an arm, flow seamlessly, one movement into the next. It was something I could do most days if not all, and it promoted healing—circulating the *chi*, the Chinese word for energy or vitality, along with the blood. As for anything more vigorous—aerobics or lifting weights—that was out for the time being. I hadn't the stamina.

What I did have was anxiety about the upcoming surgery and over the effect all this stress must be having on my immune system. It was like a dog chasing its tail. Stress was debilitating in more ways than one. Relaxing became a priority. I did breathing exercises. Inhale 2, 3, 4. Hold 2, 3, 4. Exhale 2, 3, 4. Hold 2, 3, 4 and repeat, repeat, repeat. It helped. Ten minutes of measured breathing and stillness would descend on me like nightfall, gradually extinguishing every bit of anxiety.

When I needed something more, I pulled a headset over my ears, closed my eyes, and listened to a guided meditation Gurudev recorded many years ago. It helped me to stay present in the moment and to make peace with uncertainty.

> I am not the body. It is a vehicle, a temple, and I am other than that. I reside in it. I use it. I even need it, but I am not it. Every seven years almost every cell that constitutes my body has died and been replaced by another cell. It is as if it is an entirely new thing, and yet I remain unchanged... Try now to experience yourself apart from the body. Try to feel your consciousness residing within and yet feel how it is different from the physical stuff. Experience the body as the outer most surface of your Being... Realize the body is a vehicle and not your Self...

Yes, I had a body. It was my personal means of conveyance, but like a rental car or a loaner, it was a temporary vehicle, and I knew one day it would have to be returned. For now, I was its provisional caretaker and I would do the best I could to see it restored to health. Whether my time in this body was to be short or long, my reason for being didn't change. There was a point, I had a purpose; I wanted to know God. The brain tumor and the looming surgery heightened the imperative to work harder to realize my aim.

I knew it was important for me to keep positive and so alongside the meditation and the prayer and the day-to-day efforts to be present and aware and engaged in the Work practice, I bolstered my healing resolve with affirmations. A couple of days before the surgery, I had the idea to ask others to add their resolve to my own. Science has proven the body responds to the directive to heal: mind effects body, body effects mind. So, if my solo voice singing affirmatively could help my healing, how much more potent an effect would there be with a whole chorus in the background?

From: Lorri Danzig
Subject: An invitation to collaborate...
Date: February 10, 2009 4:17:55 PM EST

To my family, friends and health caregivers,
You have been so kind these past 2 months with your prayers, healing thoughts and gifts of food, running errands and chauffeuring me to and fro. My surgery is scheduled for this Thurs. Feb 12th at 7:30 a.m.

I invite you to further collaborate with me in my healing and full recovery by supporting me with your positive affirming thoughts. Here is a suggestion of words you might say or focus on:

Affirmations
Lorri is surrounded by healing, loving energy.
Lorri's surgery will have a 100% successful outcome.
Lorri will heal completely in her own time.
Lorri will be restored to renewed strength, vitality and clarity of thought and vision.

As some of you know, after an initial 2 weeks of shock and panic following the diagnosis, I made a decision to view this benign tumor not as an enemy to be destroyed, but as a teacher, come with a teaching especially for me, a teaching I need in order to further my spiritual work. Daily, I have been meditating upon this and speaking to the tumor as a friend, letting it know I am open, ready and willing to receive its teaching. I have asked the tumor to pass the energy of its teaching on to me, that I may hold it and continue to ponder and unpack it in the months of recovery to follow.

Once the teaching is transmitted to me, this tumor/teacher understands it will no longer serve any purpose for it to exist in a physical form. I have asked the tumor/teacher to peacefully and easily relinquish its hold on my brain when Dr. Piepmeier comes for it on Thursday morning. I have asked it to go willingly into the doctor's skilled hands, without damaging any brain tissue in the process. I invite you to join me in this prayer.

Looking forward to renewing our contact after my successful surgery and recovery.
All the best,
Lorri

    I printed out the affirmations on small cards, rubber banded together a stack of about fifty of them, and placed them on my bedroom bench next to the hospital-bound gym bag that already contained pajamas, a toothbrush, my journal, and the CD from Reb Zalman. I intended to invite everyone on my Yale New Haven team to collaborate in my healing.

Lorri Danzig

Part Two

Lorri Danzig

Nine

The day before surgery Andy and I were in the kitchen cleaning up the dinner dishes when we heard a car door slam. Moments later there was a knock at the door. It was Matt and our mother. He walked in and deposited their bags on the hardwood floor with a clunk. Mom followed leaning her considerable bulk into her cane and looking a bit dazed. She wore a pair of knit pants and a print sweater that have been in her wardrobe for decades and sneakers without socks. No matter the weather, she never wore socks. I was happy she had come, but I didn't expect she would be a pillar of support. I knew this was hard for her, so soon after those months of visiting Dad everyday in the hospital. Matt had offered to sit with Andy during the surgery and I was very grateful. I expected a positive outcome. Still, surgery was surgery, and brain surgery was no tonsillectomy. There was always Moshe to think of, and if something went wrong I didn't want Andy to be facing a grim Dr. Piepmeier alone. My new friend, Cheryl, had offered to pick up Mom around noon and bring her to the hospital. There was no need for her to sit in a waiting room for hours and hours.

The conversation that evening was light. We all danced around the subject of surgery—a two-step with acceptance and a boogie with denial. In our bedroom, Andy set the alarm, checked it, and then checked it again. We had to be at the hospital by 6:30 a.m. I packed, unpacked, and repacked my duffle, afraid to leave anything important behind. In bed, Andy wrapped himself around me, and my heart beat time with his. There were no more words.

In the morning, I showered and dressed. No food or

water for me. Andy and Matt ate breakfast, and we were off. We talked and joked like carpoolers headed to work on an ordinary morning. Of the three of us, only Matt seemed tightly wound and unable to let slide the seriousness of the situation. Andy was focused on getting me to the hospital without a hitch. I wasn't nervous; I was relieved. Finally, all the anticipation was coming to an end. *In a few hours it would be done*, I thought. *Surgery over. No more tumor. On with my life.*

Andy pulled up to the valet stand at the front of the hospital. We piled out of the car. I had my small duffle. Andy carried a canvas tote bag containing his tallis, *tefillin*, prayer book, and an assortment of magazines. Matt had his laptop. At the valet stand Andy turned over his keys and I spoke to the attendant.

"Hi," I said. "I'm having brain surgery today. Would you like to join the team that is going to help me heal?"

The attendant stared at me for a moment, maybe sizing me up. Then, he smiled and said "Sure, why not. What do I have to do?"

I handed him the small card of affirmations. "Just read or say this, at 9:00 a.m. That's when they're supposed to take me in for surgery."

"Okay, will do," he said. "Good luck."

That was easy, I thought. *Onward.*

We headed for the information desk. The woman on duty pointed out where we needed to go to check-in. She too was ready and willing to become a participant in my healing. We were directed from one office to another, signing forms, answering questions. It was no wonder they made us get to the hospital so far ahead of the scheduled surgery time. There was a lot to do. All along the way, I gave out my affirmation cards. Only one person eyed me with suspicion. Maybe he thought I'd wandered out of the psych unit or maybe he was just cynical. He accepted the card, but slipped it into his pocket unread. For the smallest fraction of a second I felt a pinch of rejection, but then it passed. I was way beyond caring what some stranger thought about my plan. My very existence in a physical body felt tenuous. I was not about to waste precious energy on self-pity. Most of what we involve ourselves with is trivia. As King Solomon said in Ecclesiastes, "Vanity, vanity, all is vanity and a chasing after wind." It was taking the nearness of death for me to be able to see this clearly.

The hospital was quiet that early in the morning. Empty chairs lined most of the waiting rooms. Our last stop as a threesome was somewhere on the surgical floor. I was handed a hospital gown and sent into a curtained cubicle to change. When I gave the all clear, Andy and Matt joined me. I took a seat on the gurney, leaving the chairs for them. A nurse came in, took my blood pressure, and inserted an IV port in my arm.

"Soon," she said with a comforting nod and closed the curtain behind her as she left.

I got quiet. Fear crawled like a trail of ants, up my spine and down my arms. I forced a smile. I gripped Andy's hand. Breathe, I reminded myself. Breathe. The curtain parted again. A muscular man with ebony skin and a mop of dreadlocks pulled away from his face in a thick rubber band, greeted me. He picked up my wrist, looked at my bracelet, and then at his clipboard.

"Lorri," he said, "I'm James. I'll be taking you to the OR now."

"I was afraid of that," I said with a grin. "Can they come?" I said, not joking at all.

As James wheeled me out to the hallway, with Andy and Matt alongside, I told him all about my visualization practice, and described the images of my dad swimming me out to sea to visit the tumor and bid it adieux.

"James," I said. "Today you and your gurney get to play the role of my father the fish." James broke into a broad smile.

When we reached the swinging doors leading to the

operating room, James told Andy and Matt it was as far as they could go. Andy kissed me good-bye, Matt squeezed my hand, and I listened to their footsteps receding down the hallway.

"Will you collaborate in my healing?" I said to James, handing him a card. "Then, when the operation is a 100% success, you take some of the credit."

"Sure I will," he said. "I'd be happy to." At the door to the operating room, he stopped, walked around to the front of the gurney and smiled at me. "Good luck," he said, holding up the invitation and giving me a nod, before pushing me on through.

The room was large, much larger than I had expected, brightly lit a bluish white and crowded with monitors, stainless steel carts, and people. So many people. At least twenty, I guessed. I was expecting Dr. Piepmeier and a nurse or two, perhaps another doctor, but there were many more people, all in scrubs, one not easy to distinguish from another. Dr. Piepmeier stood off to the side with three or four others. They were looking at an MRI image on the monitor screen. Dr. Piepmeier was pointing and talking. The others nodded and conferred. He didn't seem interested that I was there. I thought he would come to speak to me or pat my arm. But he didn't. Nobody did.

Except Paul. He was a surgical nurse and part of Dr. Piepmeier's team. I liked him right away. He was reassuring, and when I explained about the affirmation cards he loved the idea. Since I wasn't going to get to talk to Dr. Piepmeier, Paul became my backup plan.

"It looks like everyone's real busy in here, so can you give them the cards for me and ask them to read them?" I said to Paul. "Also, can you ask everybody to keep the environment in here positive? No negative thoughts and especially no negative talking," I remembered an experiment described in *The Secret Life of Plants* by Peter Tompkins and Christopher Bird. A plant attached to a polygraph had reacted violently when the researcher thought about burning one of its leaves. If a philodendron's physiology could be disrupted by destructive thoughts, who knew what impact the banter of the surgical team could have on the outcome of my surgery? I wasn't going to take any chances.

"Paul," I said, "I really need this."

"No problem," he said, and I relaxed, confident he would follow through.

The anesthesiologist came over, and the moment before he sent me into La La Land, Dr. Piepmeier caught my eye, smiled, and waved.

"Relax," the anesthesiologist said. "Take a deep breath. You're going to feel a little needle..." And I was out.

A few hours later, I awoke in the recovery room. "I have the worst headache I've ever had," I announced as I came to. Andy and Matt looked at each other and cracked up. A nurse came over and upped the morphine. It worked fast, reducing the worst headache ever to a dull but persistent ache and I dozed off again.

♦♦♦

Muffled voices and loud repetitive beeps disturbed my slumber. My head hurt. I opened my eyes to bright lights and a small room with wavy walls. Andy appeared. A smiling head floating over me.

"Where am I?" I asked. Andy said I was in the recovery room. It was early afternoon. I'd been there since 11:00 a.m. He said he had been called in to see me when I first woke up, which was some time ago.

"Didn't I just wake up?" I asked, confused.

"Well, you just woke up *again*," Andy said. "You keep going in and out. But the nurse says that's normal."

"Is the tumor gone? Am I ok?"

"You did great," Andy said. "Dr. Piepmeier said he got it

127

all out."

I was relieved, then I was nauseous. Andy called the nurse. She gave me something for the queasiness and then disappeared again through the curtain. Andy placed his palm on my chest and his warmth coursed through me like a transfusion. I still felt too weak for conversation. I placed my hand on top of his, and as the nausea subsided I gave thanks to a God I hoped was listening.

Two or three nurses came in and out, checking monitors and the IV bags and asking me if I was in pain. I was never big on taking drugs of any kind, even aspirin. More often than not, I toughed out a headache rather than pop a pill, but the nurses kept telling me they didn't want me to be in pain, and I should tell them if I was. So I did, and each time they dosed me with more pain meds.

A nurse in a pretty pink top and a ponytail provided the antiemetic. I called her the Nausea Nurse. I didn't intend to be rude or funny. I knew she had told me her name before, but I found it impossible to retrieve.

"I have to get up to do tai chi," I said. "To get my energy moving, so I can heal."

Nausea Nurse laughed. "Not now, sweetie," she said. "You're not ready to stand up. You've got time for that later."

I didn't argue. I had a determined will but zero energy. Still, I did feel a sense of urgency. The surgeon had done his job, but my work was just beginning. The responsibility for recovery fell to me.

I turned to Andy. "They got it all out, right?"

Andy nodded.

"Was it benign?"

They thought so, he told me, but we had to wait for confirmation from the pathologist. It would take a little while. I was disappointed. I wanted all the uncertainty over with, yet I had to make peace with not knowing once again.

Andy placed a few of my affirmation cards on the tray

stand next to my bed. Paul, the surgical nurse, had returned them to him.

"Is this all he gave you?" I said. "That's good. It means he handed a bunch out to the surgical team like I asked." For this too, I was grateful.

Sometime later I woke up on a gurney being wheeled from the recovery room to the ICU. Andy was walking alongside me.

"Am I going to surgery now?" I asked.

"Surgery is over. You did great."

"*Yes, over*," I thought, vaguely remembering we'd had this conversation before. A heavyset man was pushing the gurney. He leaned into it, and his belly hovered over my head.

"You better quit smoking," I said. "Or you're going to end up on this gurney next."

The man raised his eyebrows at me. "Yes, ma'am, I expect you're right."

Later, Andy asked me why I would have said such a thing, and how had I known he was a smoker.

"I could hear his breathing. It didn't sound right. Somehow I knew he was a smoker, and something was wrong in his lungs. I felt it. And so I told him. For his own good." I supposed mine weren't the first set of lips to be loosened by a cocktail of morphine and steroids.

The gurney man put my bed in place and passed me off to a nurse who checked all the tubing, drip bags, and monitors. She also gave me more morphine. I opened my eyes again sometime later. Matt, Andy, and my mother were gathered around the foot of the bed, talking in not so quiet voices. Andy told me Matt had been in the recovery room with us, but I had no memory of him being there. This was the first I'd seen of my mother. She didn't say much. She looked tired and uncomfortable. I imagined she was torn between a need to be with her baby and a desire to be in her own bedroom, watching Garbo or Sinatra on TCM.

My arm hurt. It was taped to a board that was holding a

few needles in place under my skin. Each one was at the terminus of a length of tubing that ran to a bag hanging from the IV pole. One bag contained saline, the other morphine, the third, some other medication. Andy showed me how to increase the morphine drip. I shifted in the bed and the sheet caught on something. The tug sent an unexpected jolt of discomfort. Horrified, I lifted the sheet.

"Why do I have a catheter? What's wrong with my pee?"

"Nothing," Andy said. "It's just because you can't get out of bed yet."

Oh. I was resigned but not happy. My dad had a catheter after his stroke. They were for really sick people who could no longer do their own business. *Am I going to end up in that category?* And, they were invasive. I was worried that I would contract an antibiotic-resistant infection while in the hospital, and this breach of my body armor could put me at elevated risk.

I closed my eyes a lot, opening them when one nurse or another came in to poke and prod. I kept drifting off, but they didn't leave me to sleep for long. Sometimes I opened my eyes to check that I wasn't alone. I felt vulnerable, like a tree stripped of its bark. Andy was always there, usually reading an issue of *Time* or *Nature Conservancy*. My mom slept in a chair. Matt came and went, probably checking his email or calling his office. Never offline. That was him. I jealously guarded my time off the grid. My cell phone was a concession for my own safety and convenience, purchased after I had gotten lost in the backwaters of Georgia ten years before—it had been getting dark, there was no one around, and the sound track of *Deliverance* had been playing in my head. My no–frills flip-phone hibernated, powered off in the bottom of my purse unless I needed to use it. I didn't want anyone to be able to track me down every moment of the day and night.

That night, Andy sent an email to our friends and family.

My Father the Fish

From: Andy Danzig
Subject: Lorri update
Date: February 12, 2009 9:34:08 PM EST

Lorri's surgery went extremely well today, thank G-d. The procedure lasted about 2 hours. The drs report removing the whole tumor.

She awoke from anesthesia with the biggest headache she's ever had. But it's being controlled with morphine. It didn't stop her from lecturing one of the surgical residents on the importance of treating patients as whole beings not as a car that needs parts replaced. If you thought Lorri waxed philosophic before, she picked up where she left off right out of the gate. It's an amazing sight and even more beautiful to hear.

She passed out cards containing the affirmations in her last email to everyone she engaged at the hospital, from the parking attendant to gurney drivers to nurses and of course, her surgical team and post-op caregivers. The quality of care received at Yale Hospital so far has been exemplary, which gave us comfort to take leave for the night. She's being fed liquids tonight: broth, jello, etc. and should be fed solid food tomorrow. She should be out of ICU tomorrow also.

That's all for now, still lots to do at home. Thanks for all your calls, concerns and continued prayers.
Love, Andy

I didn't get to see his email until sometime later, and when I did, I beamed. It pulsed with his love and admiration. There was so much to be grateful for.

While he was sending his email from home, I drifted in and out of sleep. The nurses woke me at regular intervals to do a neuro-check (the now familiar routine of beaming a flashlight into my eyes) and to check my vital signs. Early Friday morning, I had a seizure. It was not like the ones that landed me in the ER two months earlier. This seizure had me flopping like a flounder. It started in my right arm. I had just managed to push the call button when my left arm, and then my whole body, started to bounce. I didn't lose consciousness, I flailed about. I couldn't stop it. *Call the exorcist*, I thought. But the nurse, who had arrived in seconds, kept me from falling off the bed and called a doctor. He ordered more meds. No one gave me any pills so I guessed they were being delivered through one of the IVs. The seizing subsided but not my terror. What the hell was that all about? The tumor was gone. I was supposed to be better. Then, I remembered Moshe. *Oh shit*, I thought, *maybe my brain got nicked or something during the surgery*. But, the on-call doctor told me the seizure was most likely due to postsurgical swelling of my brain and not to any new damage. Nonetheless, they wheeled me off for a CAT scan and I remembered nothing more. Maybe I fell asleep again.

Andy was back later Friday morning. He came with me when I was wheeled down for an EEG—something to do with the early morning seizure. Later, Dr. Piepmeier would tell me the test was pointless because the EEG would only show brainwave disturbance while I was in the throes of the seizure, not six hours afterward. I wondered who had ordered the EEG, and why didn't they didn't know what Dr. Piepmeier knew? But at the time of the testing, I was in the dark about all that and just went along.

"I can't do it with that on you," the technician said. "They should have taken it off."

"What?" I said, clueless.

"You got a mirror?" Andy asked. And she reached over and handed him one, which he held in front of my face.

"Wow," was all I could say. My head was wrapped in gauze bandages. Wrapped and wrapped and wrapped. I had a large turban on my head. "I look like a Sikh." I guess I should have realized there would be a bandage, but I had been conscientiously avoiding touching my head. The thought of my skull, which had been sawed through, opened up, and fastened back together, made me squeamish. I found it preferable to ignore or disown it altogether.

A doctor, or maybe it was a nurse, arrived and unwrapped the bandages. The technician stuck perhaps a dozen gooey little round tabs all over my skull. Each was connected to a wire running to the EEG machine. Again, Andy provided the mirror. *A bride for Frankenstein's monster*, I thought. My eyes were puffy and I had bloody scabs and indentations on my temples and forehead from the clamps that had immobilized my head during the surgery. I couldn't see the site of the incision, which was probably a good thing. Andy said it was six inches long and held together by staples. *Staples, not stitches?* I thought. *Like what? Carpet tacks?* I looked a sight. A large patch of hair on my crown had been cropped short, but at least they hadn't shaved my head.

The EEG testing took a long time. I had to lie very still, and I was bored. Andy chatted with the technician but I couldn't hear them. After the EEG I was wheeled to my room up on the 6th floor. I got to eat some oatmeal and later in the day rice and beans, which I ordered off the menu. I was afraid to eat too much because what was going in was not coming out. Though tired, I couldn't sleep for long. I rested. Andy read a back issue of *Sierra* magazine. I stirred when a man I took to be a doctor entered the room. I didn't remember him but then there had been so many doctors, so

133

many nurses. Every shift change brought new faces. He responded to my greeting and came over to the bed and smiled.

"How are you doing today, young lady?" He said.

I took this as an invitation and an opportunity to share how well I was doing, which was pretty great, considering. I was sure all the prayers and the affirmations were responsible.

"I call that the power of love," he said, and we two were off and running, exploring the role of prayer in healing and the strength of a positive attitude. "Well, I best be getting about my work," he said at last.

I expected him to exit and continue making his rounds. But no. He walked over to the heating unit at the rear of the room and unscrewed the cover.

"What work do you do?" I called over to him.

"Well, he said, I do God's work. I'm a minister at a church down here in New Haven. But today I'm cleaning radiators."

During one of my naps a nurse or technician removed the catheter. I woke up and saw it was gone. I didn't remember it being removed, just as I had no memory of it being inserted. I was relieved on both counts. The very word *catheter* made my skin crawl.

Two nurses came to get me out of bed. My balance was awful and I couldn't walk on my own. Still, I was amazed. Twenty-four hours after brain surgery and I was up and about with a nurse supporting me on either side. My mother and Matt came again to visit later in the day, and my friend Sarah stopped in on her way to work. I didn't have much energy for anyone. I talked little and napped a lot. I was being given painkillers at regular intervals and was comfortable enough. By evening I pushed aside the little plastic cup holding my pain medication. That turned out to be a mistake. The pain came back, big time. I didn't refuse any more pills.

Close to 4:00 p.m., as daylight was waning, I sent Andy

home. I didn't want him to get stuck at the hospital overnight. On Friday afternoons, the sun dropping below the horizon ushered in the Sabbath, and Andy hung up his car keys for twenty-five hours. Matt and Mom said they would stay with me longer, but they both looked tired and so was I. My head throbbed. It was time for me to go offline, so I sent them home too. I wasn't afraid anymore. I knew I was healing. I could feel it. I wanted to listen to my CD from Reb Zalman and I wanted to sleep.

Ten

The first time I peed without the catheter it burned, but what a relief to be doing my business on my own. Still, nurses kept my bladder situation under close surveillance. Every so often a nurse came in and ran an ultrasound wand over my belly. It showed how full my bladder was. "If you can't empty your bladder we will have to catheterize you again," the nurse told me. I winced. A catheter wasn't so bad, she told me. *Right.* I thought. *Not so bad for you.*

I wasn't peeing enough. Why I couldn't pee I didn't know. At first I drank a lot because I thought this would make me pee, but then when it didn't, I stopped drinking altogether.

Later in the evening, after a shift change, Nurse Jesse arrived in my room to check on me. He walked me to the bathroom and afterwards, like the nurses earlier, wanded my bladder. He was not happy with the results, but rather than threaten me with another catheter, he took another tack.

"Here's what you have to do," he said. "Walk. I'll help you. Walking will make you pee."

He helped me sit up and secured the walker for me while I swung my legs out of the bed and grasped hold. He positioned the IV pole off to the side and a little in front of me and off we went out the door. I pushed the walker. He pushed the IV pole. I walked the distance of two rooms and stopped. "A little more, you can do it," he encouraged, like a personal trainer. Returning to my room he led me straight into the bathroom and stood outside the door while I peed. *Success*, I thought.

He got me back in bed and checked my bladder. It was

still half full. Too full, he told me. I sighed. He let me rest for a while and then had me up and walking again. Walk, pee, repeat. When my bladder was emptied to his professional satisfaction, he let me go back to sleep. In the morning he was gone. His shift had ended before I woke.

As soon as I was out of the hospital I wrote a thank you letter to Jesse and to two other nurses who had cared for me. Jesse responded. "Your words of encouragement have made me feel special and worthwhile for being a nurse." It was indeed the small things that mattered so much. I had felt so vulnerable as a patient after receiving misinformation about my diagnosis, being prescribed blood thinners I hadn't needed, and subjected to a useless EEG. To these particular nurses I was not just a name on the hospital ID bracelet and a body to be administered to according to protocol. They ministered to all my needs, not only the ones they were monitoring with all the high tech equipment. I was kiss-the-ground grateful. I learned later, because of my letters, all three were awarded special recognition as Nurse of the Month, and that made me very happy.

Well before 6 a.m. that Saturday morning, I pushed my walker, unassisted, down a hushed hallway. A few nurses sat at a nursing station writing in patients' charts or typing on a keyboard. Two white-coated doctors, stethoscopes around their necks, conferred in soft voices. I looked into each room as I passed. A few TVs were on. Most patients were still sleeping. It was too early for visitors.

"Well, look at you." A voice came at me from the end of the hall. I turned to find Dr. Piepmeier walking in my direction. "How are you feeling?"

"Pretty good," I said, flashing a broad smile.

"Would you like to go home today?" he asked.

"Home? Am I ready?" Not quite 48 hours post-op, it seemed incredible I could leave the hospital so soon.

"I reviewed your chart and you look great. I have no medical reason to keep you here," he said. "But you must make sure to get yourself up and walking." He paused and smiled. "I don't see a problem there. You look motivated to me."

Well, of course I wanted to go home. Hospitals were hotbeds of infection, and I wanted to get out of there as soon as possible. There was no antibiotic-resistant staph lurking on my kitchen countertops; at home the resident germs and I had a long-standing relationship and I had built a natural immunity. Dr. Piepmeier told me there was no rush. I could stay all day if I wanted to. It would take hours to get all the discharge papers ready in any case.

Then, almost as an afterthought, he added, "By the way, the pathology report came back. We have confirmation that the tumor was benign."

I shuffled to my bed, elated. Benign for sure and going home. Now I could really start to mend. I listened to Reb Zalman again. "Ana El na, refa na la," he sang. "Please God, heal her." The prayers were working. I fell back to sleep and when I awoke a physical therapist stood jotting in a file at the foot of my bed. She had to assess me before I could be discharged. Dr. Piepmeier had said I could go home, but it seemed there were some tests I would have to pass before that could happen. The physical therapist had me up and walking without the walker. Leaning into her, I teetered back and forth down the hall, each step tentative and wobbly. She led me to a stairwell. There were six steps up to a landing. Not too steep, but even with her help I couldn't do the stairs. Not even one. That worried me. *Will I be here another night after all?* But no, since I lived in a ranch, stairs weren't a deal breaker. I could still go home. She ordered a walker for me to take home and also wrote out orders for outpatient physical therapy I could begin in a week or so.

"Why can't I keep my balance?" I asked. She explained there were one or possibly two things going on. For sure, my brain was very swollen and the pressure could be affecting my ability to balance, and there could be some brain damage. My eyes widened. But that, she assured, could be overcome in time with physical therapy. The brain is versatile she explained, and skills can be retaught and learned by undamaged brain cells. I let out my breath. After the PT assessment there were more nurses' visits, more paperwork, more check-ins by doctors on-duty.

It had been a busy morning and I was tired out. I called home, knowing Andy would be at shul. Matt answered the phone. I told him the doctor said I could go home any time. He said he would pick me up so I didn't have to wait for Andy to come after sundown when Shabbat was over.

"Good," I said. "But don't come now. I'll call you later. When I'm ready."

But he did come. And that was a disaster for me. Matt is a no-nonsense sort of guy. He is super-efficient and likes to always be one step ahead of the game. He moves very fast and can be very impatient. That was not what I needed. He showed up around 11 a.m. and in a whirlwind began packing up my stuff. Though I knew he was trying to be helpful, it was more help than I could tolerate. I was so tired. I felt pressured to snap to it and get out the door. Physically, I couldn't do it.

"Matt. Please leave everything," I said. "Wait outside. I'll let you know when I'm ready to go."

It was not something I would have done before. I would have been too afraid of hurting his feelings. I knew he was trying to help; he had been there for me and for Andy throughout this ordeal, but just then none of that mattered. I'd had brain surgery. I could have ended up like Moshe. I could have died. In the face of all those, thank God, un-actualized possibilities, whether I appeared well-mannered and sufficiently appreciative or not, was of no consequence to me. My priority was getting well. I had this body to think of, to care for, and that mattered more to me in that moment than Matt's reaction or his opinion of me.

I held to the Jewish teaching, that my body was on loan

from God, and I had a fiduciary responsibility to care for it. I was not a property owner. I was akin to a caretaker expected to execute that role with diligence. This made infinite sense to me, and right then I was taking the edict very seriously. As soon as Matt left the room I began unpacking my duffle again. I wanted my book, my journal, and Reb Zalman's CD within easy reach. Though not edible they were, in essence, my comfort foods. They fed my soul. I climbed into bed, pulled up the covers and drifted off to *Ana, El na, refa na la*. I was so tired.

    Matt and I left the hospital later in the afternoon with a walker, discharge instructions, and prescriptions to be filled: Keppra, painkillers, steroids (to reduce brain swelling), and a stool softener. A hospital volunteer pushed me in a wheelchair while Matt made a beeline for the lobby. He steam-rolled through the halls with my duffle and god help anyone in his path.

    There was more than one route home. If we traveled down Whalley Avenue we would pass by a Walgreens. I suggested to Matt that we make the stop so he wouldn't have to run out again to fill my prescriptions. This was not a good idea and flew in the face of my plan to listen to my body which was exhausted and screaming to be put to bed. So why did I suggest it?

    Sleep. The Watcher had slumped down in her balcony seat and nodded off. So, there was no awareness that the part of me that wanted to be seen as a real trouper, and not a whiny weakling, had pushed her way out onto center stage. Unobserved, she was able to improvise her lines and perform them without interference. This is why the Watcher can not be permitted even a little catnap. The briefest snooze could spell disaster. A wakeful Watcher would have seen at least two actors, the trouper and the whiny weakling, competing for the spotlight. She would have recognized them for what they both were: inconsequential aspects of personality each with an agenda at odds with Lorri's spiritual aim and with her plan for self-care. That awareness alone would have allowed for a course of action governed by reason.

But as I said, that's not how the scene played out. We stopped at Walgreen's. I had expected a ten minute wait in the car. *Ten minutes is nothing,* I thought. *I'll just close my eyes and rest.* But the pharmacists were busy and a half hour passed before Matt reappeared. I was cold and uncomfortable and more tired than I could ever remember being. *Wake up!* I said to myself, as Matt turned the car toward home. This wanting to be liked and to be seen as strong and independent could be the death of me, spiritually for sure, and quite possibly physically as well if I didn't let myself heal. I didn't like the picture of a Lorri who was weak and disabled. But that's what I was... for the time being. I was not going to be able to go home and pick up where I left off six weeks earlier. I was going to need a lot of help. I would have to ask for it and accept it.

We pulled up to the house, and Matt helped me out of the car. My legs shook from exhaustion and weakness. I leaned into the walker and inched up the path. Ten more yards. Only ten more yards. I felt like a mountain climber clawing my way to the summit after a brutal ascent. Once inside I greeted my mom and then headed straight for my bedroom. I wanted quiet, I wanted something to eat, and I wanted to rest.

♦♦♦

In the late afternoon light, my bedroom was a soft gold. Only a year before, I had painted the walls yellow and replaced the rose-colored rug with a pale yellow carpet. The rug had been there when we moved into the house. It had always made me feel unwell in some way I couldn't pinpoint. I was grateful we had ripped it up. I was sure having it under my feet now would have impeded my healing. The yellow cloud that surrounded me was as soothing as sunshine.

All around me were healing talismans and tokens of love. A wicker basket overflowed with get-well cards, and a short stack of books waited to entertain and educate me. Taped to the headboard above my bed was a series of four panels drawn by Andy's cousin Lisi, an artist. With bold strokes of black on white paper she had combined reiki and Kabbalistic symbols with Hebrew lettering. The note she tucked in with the drawings said they would promote healing. Hanging over my night table was a colorful rendering of a round-eyed fish, a gift from Rosalie, my sage-ing friend. Beneath the picture, she captured the tale of my father the fish in just four lines:

> The fish is carrying me on its back,
> Swimming through my skull.
> Swishing healing mikveh waters,
> Around my brain.

An amethyst crystal danced in front of the window. The refracted light cast a rainbow on the coverlet. The crystal was a gift from a friend of a friend, who also had a meningioma. She had had two surgeries but still had symptoms and occasional seizures. I called her after I was diagnosed. I wasn't sure what I was hoping for, but she had walked in my shoes as no one else I knew had. That first time we spoke, I guess she thought I needed information, the straight facts on what to expect. My breath stuck in my chest as she unraveled possible best- and worst-case scenarios, listed questions I should ask of doctors, and outlined the decisions I would be asked to make. I got off the phone feeling shell-shocked.

Years later I would read a blog post by Kendra Peterson, a neurologist in Palo Alto. She cautioned that the details of life-threatening or life-changing diagnoses often needed to be meted out to patients piecemeal rather than dumped on the table all at once. That was certainly true in my case. I would have benefited from a smaller helping of truth until I could digest the bigger picture. Still, I called her again a couple of weeks later when I felt down and then I was grateful for her listening heart. She emailed often and responded quickly whenever I contacted her. When I worried over a symptom, she consoled me. When I voiced my fears of what would be after the surgery, she reassured me. She was a strong link in my network of support, and yet she had been little more than a stranger when I made that first phone call.

There were only a few people in my life I called friends, but my community was populated by many more concerned acquaintances than I had ever imagined. I took great comfort in that. In the hospital there were doctors and nurses watching over me. What if something happened here at home? The incision reopened? A seizure? Bleeding? I didn't know what to expect. My head throbbed, keeping time with the thumping in my chest. In the hospital I felt powerless, at risk of infection, complications, and doctor error. Now I was home where I wanted to be, but I didn't feel safe here either.

Pushing the walker in front of me, I baby-stepped into my bathroom and stood in front of the vanity. *Mirror, mirror on the wall, who's the fairest of them all?* For sure, not me. The dents on my forehead and temples were an angry red. My hair stood out in small clumps of gooey post-op punk. I angled a hand mirror but I still couldn't get a good view of my incision. Very gently, I ran my fingers over the bristles on the crown of my head and traced the staple line. The sensation made me nauseous. I steadied myself on the walker before returning to the bedroom and folding onto the bed.

Andy returned from shul while I was resting. He brought me a cup of tea and leftover soup and sat down on the bed.

"I'm so glad to have you home," he said. "I straightened out the mess with your pills. It's being taken care of." The pharmacy had filled my prescription per the script signed by Dr. Gardiner, but the discharge instructions signed by a different doctor indicated a different dosage. The right hand didn't know what the left hand was doing. I had expected a medical *team*, but there was no teamwork. With each shift change there had been a new doctor, and I feared communication between them was about as effective as a game of telephone.

"Do I have to take anything now?" I asked Andy. No, the next pill wouldn't be for a couple of hours. "I need to make a chart. To keep track of when to take what." I was hyper-vigilant when it came to taking medications. If the dose was supposed to go down the hatch at 4:00 p.m., then 4:00 p.m. it would be. Not 3:50 p.m. or 4:15 p.m. I was sifting through my night table drawer for a piece of paper and a pencil when my hands flew up to my head and gripped my crown. Eyes wide, I grimaced.

"What is it?" Andy said with alarm.

I was dizzy and a little nauseous. Andy made a move towards me and I closed my eyes.

"Don't move." I ordered.

"What's the..."

"Don't talk," I whispered. And I sat holding my head trying very hard not to panic. Breathe, I thought. Just breathe.

A couple of minutes passed and Andy tried again. "Lor?"

I lowered my arms and opened my eyes a slit. "It's my head," I said. "It's... it's *wonging*."

"Wonging?" he said.

I didn't know what to call it, this unbearable not-pain inside my head like the reverberations of a temple gong. Wongggggggggg. Wongggggggggg.

"Do you think something's gone wrong?" I asked.

"I don't know," Andy said. "Is it still happening?"

"It's subsiding a little. I think I need to sleep now," I said, sliding down under the covers. I turned onto my side and curled up knees-to-chest, head-to-knees. But I didn't sleep.

Eleven

"Toilet won't flush," Andy announced as he exited the bathroom. "Be right back, I'll get the plunger."

Great, I thought. *One day out of the hospital, three houseguests, and a clogged toilet.*

Our plumbing had a habit of breaking down whenever we had visitors. This time though, the Murphy of Murphy's Law had outdone himself. It was a Sunday. When the plunger failed to bring results, I insisted Andy call Eric, his aikido buddy who had known about Dr. Piepmeier. Eric was a plumber and a really good guy. He showed up within a couple of hours, performed a cursory examination of the toilet, and pronounced the patient dead. He and Andy made a run to Lowe's and returned within the hour with a new toilet and some PVC fittings. Though I was appreciative of Eric giving up his Sunday to come fix my toilet, what I really wanted was peace and quiet. What I got was a lot of banging and clamoring not five feet from the foot of my bed.

The bathroom was small, and the door had to remain open to give Eric and Andy room to maneuver in such a tight space. Eric avoided making eye contact with me when he reached out of the bathroom to grab a tool or a piece of pipe from the bedroom floor. "Sorry. Excuse me," he said. I didn't know Eric well at all. The handful of times I'd talked to him he was not shy, but polite and respectful, in an old-school way. His intrusion into my sickroom seemed to embarrass him. I, on the other hand, was glad it was Eric in eyeshot and not some plumber with a beer belly and low-slung pants that Andy had picked at random out of the Yellow Pages.

It took Eric and Andy a few hours, but at last I heard the

flush of success.

"Done." Eric said, this time meeting my eyes with a smile. I was so grateful it was fixed, and now I would have my room back to myself. I thanked Eric for coming to our rescue and could have left it at that, but I didn't. He for sure wasn't expecting polite small talk from me—I'd just had brain surgery for god's sake—and small talk is not what he got. Without so much as a segue, I went from plumbing to poking and prodding at Eric's psyche. His son had been killed in a car accident a year or so before, and Andy had told me Eric was still devastated.

"Eric," I said. "I know your son's death left you with a hole in your heart, but it's time to fill in that hole and plant a garden. Let some beauty into your life again."

Eric looked away.

Andy's eyes were wide. He looked straight at me and shook his head from side to side in small almost imperceptible movements.

Stop? I thought. *Why?* And so I continued.

"Eric, I see you in the future. And you are healed and at peace." Now I was an oracle, too.

Eric murmured something and Andy hurried him out of our bedroom.

"What?" I shrugged.

I was reading when Andy returned a few minutes later. "Why would you say that to Eric?" Andy said. "You know he doesn't want to go there."

I didn't see what the problem was. I thought I'd done a good thing. I was trying to show Eric a way out from his pain. Andy let it go. He wasn't going to argue with me—not then.

"Send Matt in," I said. "I'll speak to him now." I sat up taller in the bed and waited for him to appear. I allowed for the pleasantries—how are you feeling? Not bad, considering, and so on—then, without invitation, I deconstructed Matt's relationship problems in excruciating detail. Since I thought I had all the answers, I offered advice. Matt seemed to fall under my spell. At least he didn't back out of the room. He listened, taking in every word, and it seemed he was open to what I had to say. When I was through, I dismissed him, and he returned to the living room where, he would tell me later, he, Andy, and Debbie all had a good laugh over the way I was playing the queen, granting audience to my subjects.

Alone again, I surveyed the room: quilted throw pillows piled on the bench, a Japanese watercolor, and several issues of *Time* on Andy's night table. I was preternaturally calm. Anxious is my baseline state, and this mellow state should have felt weird, but it didn't. I was like a lioness, top of the food chain, nothing to fear. "Come in," I said to the knock at the door. Debbie entered carrying a pill bottle and a glass of water. She had arrived that morning and taken up her role as resident nurse.

"Time for these," she said, setting the glass down on the night table and doling out a capsule. Debbie's presence in the house was a godsend. "Let me take a look," she said, tipping my head down and inspecting the incision. "Looking good," she said, and I believed her. Where I would write off Andy's reassurances as hopeful optimism, her words carried all the weight of her years of experience as a floor nurse. She knew what healing looked like.

"Did you go yet?" she asked.

"Uh, uh," I nodded. "I'm really uncomfortable, too."

"These doctors!" she said, eyeing the bottle of stool softeners. "They don't have a clue what actually works! Where's there a drugstore? I gotta get you something." Debbie was out the door and back again in less than twenty minutes. She handed me a small jar of Fleet glycerin suppositories. "Try this," she said.

Judaism, the religion with a blessing for everything, has a prayer one recites after a productive trip to the bathroom. A rough translation goes like this:

> Blessed are You, oh Lord our God, who created me in miraculous ways, with all sorts of hollows and ducts and inner organs. If any of those hollows should clog, ducts malfunction, or organs seep, I could not exist in Your Presence for even a moment. Thank you, God, for healing me in miraculous ways.

I call it "the bathroom prayer," but only that afternoon did I come to appreciate how important a blessing it was. "Hallelujah," I sang out from the bathroom only fifteen minutes later.

With Debbie in the house I was more relaxed. She eased the transition from the round-the-clock watchful eye of the hospital staff to my own bed at home. That she was my personal Florence Nightingale did not mean she escaped my penchant for truth-telling that day. Debbie's habit of ridiculing Andy's religious practice set me on edge, though Andy shrugged off her digs and sarcasm. That's Debbie for you, he'd say. Despite his equanimity, I felt protective of him, whether he needed protecting or not. Andy was committed to do as he did because he believed it was what God wanted of him and that by following God's way, he would draw closer to God. I loved Andy and, from where I sat on my throne that day, I wasn't about to tolerate any arrows flying in his direction.

"Deb," I said, "I know Andy can be annoying."

He gets all frazzled if the sun has set and the Shabbat candles haven't been lit, or a dairy spoon has found its way into a drawer with meat forks. Debbie thinks he's crazy for walking to shul in all kinds of weather and sitting in the dark rather than flicking on a light switch, but this is his practice and, I reminded her, he didn't invent it. He follows Torah law.

Being Torah observant was no trivial pursuit for Andy. It was the way he expressed his relationship to God. He was both committed and disciplined. Andy carried out his practice between two pillars of do's and don'ts that on the surface appeared to me as little more than an elaborate moral construct. But I knew Judaism was rooted in profound truths about God, man, and man's purpose in relation to God. Andy seemed to be most engaged in exploring the leaves and branches that made up the visible structure of Judaism and had little practical interest as yet in the roots that hid and flourished beneath the surface. I continued to hope that one day he would turn his attention to the deeper work.

"Debbie, you don't have to value his way of being Jewish," I said. "But you don't have to deride him for it either. It's painful." I was sure Debbie took what I said to mean her behavior hurt Andy, but really, that was not quite true. He didn't appreciate her barbs, but I was the one that suffered her words, and it was my heart I was protecting from further assault.

Debbie did not defend against my pointed critique. "You've given me a glimpse of Andy in a different light," she said. "Thank you for that."

I didn't respond. I had heard enough and I was too caught up with myself to have any interest in entering into a dialogue.

Debbie pocketed the pill bottle, picked up the glass, and then hesitated at the door.

"Your mom wants to know why she can't come in to see you," Debbie said. "You should let her in. She's feeling rejected, and she's going home today."

That morning I had told Andy I didn't want people in and out of my room. I wanted quiet and privacy. I would tell him who could come in, and I had been avoiding my mother. She was dealing with my surgery about as well as she had dealt with my father's stroke, which was to say not dealing well at all, and I didn't have the energy or the inclination to try and make her feel better. She seemed pretty much numb. Maybe seeing me in the hospital was too much for her and maybe she was simply exhausted: emotionally and physically. In any case, so was I, but I couldn't ignore what Debbie had told me. My mom had never been the nurturing, chicken-soup-ladling sort of mom, but she had schlepped all the way up here from Long Island to be with me and that in itself was a big show of support. "Debbie," I said, "ask her to come in."

Mom shuffled, leaning heavily on her cane. She looked very tired and so old. When did that happen, the deep furrows and drooping folds of the jowls? My mom had always had great skin. I waited until she settled herself in the chair by my bed and then I began speaking about my dad. She had once told me it was a great consolation to her when she ran into folks who had known him and would speak of him to her. It brought him back to life in a way. It reconnected her to the years where her richest memories lay. But that was not why I brought him up. I wasn't concerning myself with her needs. Stripped as I was of all inhibition, I spoke my mind, whatever was on it.

I had not had the kind of relationship I wanted with my dad. I had yearned for an intimacy that was never there. My father loved me, and I always knew that, but it felt like a kind of generic love of a father for a daughter. I didn't feel he knew or understood me as a grown-up person who was no longer Daddy's little girl. He was just as much of a mystery to me. Sometime during my teens an invisible barrier had grown up between us, and it remained standing until after the stroke that led to his death three months later. Though the stroke left him speechless, we at last communicated heart to heart, eye to eye, and with a touch of a hand.

The intimacy between us had been birthed in silence and had grown over the past few weeks during his visits to me in the guise of a fish. My mom listened to my description of Daddy carrying me out to sea to address the tumor. The absence of skepticism on her part did not surprise me. After my dad died, Mom told me she would wake up at night feeling his arms wrapped around her, his chest pressing into her back. She saw a light body in the shape of his form lying next to her in their bed. She didn't question it was him, whatever "him" might have meant after the death of the body, so my story was well within the realm of her understanding.

"Without Daddy being with me," I said, "I don't know how I would have gotten through all this. I was so scared."

Mom took my hand, tears washing her cheeks. We both reached for the tissue box.

Then without inhibition or reservation, ready to cross all boundaries, I ventured onto turf I had avoided for over thirty years. I had never told my mom I'd felt abandoned by her and Dad when I had lived in the ashram as Gurudev's disciple.

"I was very hurt," I said. "You and Daddy were so wrapped up in your fears, I was invisible to you."

"We were terrified," Mom said. "We thought we'd lost you forever."

"But you hadn't and you didn't listen to me. You didn't see *me*."

I had been, despite their gravest fears and wildest imaginings, living a productive life. I wasn't doing drugs, or other women's husbands, I was in good health, had a responsible job, nice clothes, and a car at my disposal when I wanted to visit them. Yet, they had remained convinced I had been brainwashed and was being held against my will and forced to do God knows what.

Late afternoon sunlight trickled through my bedroom window. In the dim light, Mom and I sat together in silence. She reached for my hand. There were no apologies just, I imagined, a shared feeling of loss. For me, there was catharsis. I had ached to tell my parents how betrayed I had felt. But I never had. I was not one to stir the pot. Once I had regained my place in their universe as a shining star, I had avoided turning their attention back to that period that had been excruciating for us all.

My return to my parents' good graces had come long after Gurudev had disbanded the ashram. It was time, he had said, for us disciples to stand on our own two feet as competent adults and householders. He had seen too many "enlightened" yogis leave their cave in India, only to fall apart spiritually when encountering the wider world. In 1993, a few other disciples and I followed Gurudev and his family to Maui. There, we lived much like other people. I had a management position in our dietary supplement business, an excellent salary, my own car, a to-die-for house overlooking the Pacific, and yes… health insurance. The thing was, from my perspective nothing much about my life had changed. I still engaged in the same spiritual practices, applied the same principles to the living of my life, and wrote my "driver analysis", which by that time was written in a Word document I emailed to Gurudev each night for comment. Only on the surface did my life appear different from the ashram days, but the surface was all my parents had ever been able to see. They had never gotten to know Dr. Sohn, my Gurudev—not so much as a conversation in all the years.

On one amazing day, almost twenty years after I had become Gurudev's student, my parents took their blinders off. They had been visiting me in Maui, and I had given them a tour of Sustainable Technologies, Inc., the bio-converter start-up that was one of the business operations I helped oversee. I explained how the strain of bacteria living inside the silo-like bio-converter digested the fats, oils, and grease and other food waste provided by restaurants and hotels around the island.

"The end products are methane and hydrogen gas, sources of clean energy, and also a high quality organic fertilizer." I said.

"We're so proud of you," my father said.

"Yes," said Mom. "You have grown so much over the years. We hardly recognize you. So accomplished. So much self-confidence. Not the same girl you used to be."

"You are so happy and are doing so well," said Dad. "I guess Dr. Sohn has been good for you."

Mom nodded in agreement.

I never thought I would hear those words. After that, our relationship changed. Chances are they hadn't even noticed, but for me, their affirmation went a long way toward bringing down the wall that had stood between us. Opening up to my mom about how rejected I had felt all those years ago brought the last stones tumbling to the ground. I wasn't looking for an apology from her. I didn't need it. I understood her pain by then and had compassion for her. But I did need to be heard, to stand up and be counted, and in doing so I carved a space in myself into which forgiveness could flow.

My mother was my last visitor of the afternoon. The queen was ready to retire. It had been a wild day so far. My behavior, as it turned out, was a not uncommon withdrawal response from dexamethasone, a corticosteroid I had been taking to reduce the swelling in my brain. This same drug had gained notoriety in professional sports where athletes were taking it to enhance performance. I totally got it. I felt like Superman—able to leap tall buildings at a single bound, more powerful than a locomotive, and yet all the while, my energy level was very low. I was a bundle of contradictions and my behavior was very strange.

All the truth telling wore me out. I was tired anyway. Whether lying in bed or propped up in the recliner, I couldn't sleep for more than two hours at a time. I could not take any pressure, not even a pillow, against my head. The previous night the pain had built until it woke me up, and then I was counting down the clock until I could take more painkillers.

Later in the afternoon, when Andy came in to take a nap, I wandered into my temple room. I called it that because, like the ashram's temple, it was intended as a sanctuary. There, I could meditate, reflect, read, and write undisturbed. I had staked my claim on the spare room when we first moved into the house in Woodbridge. "I need a space of my own," I had told Andy.

Walking through the door of the ashram's temple was like stepping into sunshine after a rainstorm has scrubbed the air of all dust and pollen leaving behind low humidity and impossibly vibrant colors. The temple tingled with spiritual energy. My temple room failed to produce such a charged atmosphere, but it did afford me the quiet and alone time I coveted. I guarded the sanctity of my small room, though it bore little resemblance to the ashram's spacious temple. There, dormer windows channeled the light that illuminated the paintings of Hindu deities and hand-lettered aphorisms that covered the sloping walls as reminders to the spiritual aspirant of the principles of the Work. At the front of the temple, on a raised platform covered with a Persian rug and flanked by man-size houseplants, sat a massive bronze statue of the god Shiva, the destroyer of illusion, in a ring of flames. Nearby were smaller statues of Hindu deities, a Christian crucifix atop a six foot pole, and a brass menorah. A large portrait of Gurudev's grandfather, an observant Jew and his first spiritual teacher, hung in an alcove. Meditation pillows were lined up in neat rows on the pale blue carpet. There was no furniture.

My temple room was small. Three bookcases held volumes on quantum physics, Samkhya yoga, Gurdjieff's Fourth Way, and other philosophical and religious treatises. My yoga mat and meditation pillow were stowed in a corner of the room. On a low shelf, eye level when I sat on the floor, I had on display photographs of Gurudev, Reb Zalman, and Roshi Joan Halifax, a Zen priest who had taught me how to be fully present with my dad while he was dying. An old desk, an oak chair, and a leather recliner were the only other furniture. The terracotta walls were backdrop to three black and white photographs of Gurudev demonstrating tai chi, the immovable stance, and other feats of physical and energetic control. An etching of an old rabbi studying Talmud, Gurudev's words on faith, hope and love, and my *ketuba*—Jewish marriage certificate—hung over my desk.

Sinking into the cool leather of the recliner, I settled my Mac onto my lap and began to sift through the many days of unread email. Andy had copied me on the notes he had sent to friends and family over the past several days. In one, he commented on a conversation he had with the EEG technician. He wrote: "Unless you engage the person who's standing next to you, or is in your presence for whatever reason, you're missing an opportunity to create a relationship, which not only fosters understanding of another, but offers incredible opportunity to learn something new."

I knew Andy. He did not tend to wax philosophic, so this excerpt from his conversation caught my attention. His words were quietly bursting with a joy of discovery. I recognized it as being like the joy I felt when a flash of insight illuminated my world. He had, I thought, made a connection to a deeper possibility and was very excited by it.

When I had asked my brother-in-law David to speak with Andy and let him know how much I needed his support, it was because much of the time I saw Andy as unwilling, or at least resistant to, climbing into my skin and seeing the world as I saw it. It was not a matter of my perspective being any better or clearer than his, but because for him to really understand me he had to see my world from my point of view, or as the Cherokee proverb put it, he had to walk a mile in my moccasins.

Although Andy and I shared a deep love and connection, I often felt there was a wall between us—not a dense impenetrable wall of stone, but rather one made of Plexiglas. I could see him, he could see me, but I couldn't feel his touch. To a large extent I felt the wall was built of his unwillingness to consider the world—a world that included

155

me—from any perspective but his own. So many times I had accused him of not seeing me, but only his pictures of me. How can there be relationship without understanding of "the other"? Perhaps I was reading more into his email than was really there, but at the time I believed the thoughts he shared on his encounter with the EEG tech were an aha! moment for him. I thought he finally understood what the Cherokees were getting at, and the implications for the future of our relationship were enormous. The force of his words had punched a hole in the wall that I perceived standing between us. My tears came rushing through.

I continued to peruse his emails. He wrote, "…up and walking, eating, and being discharged a full day before expected. She's unsteady on her feet so walks with a walker, but the important thing is, SHE'S HOME!!" He closed with what he referred to as "an administrative detail," that for me was more reflective of ministration than administration. "She's sensitive to sounds and stimulation," he wrote, "so don't rush over to see her or call her. As her energy level improves, she'll be in touch." The sensitivity he talked about was the wonging. It happened often and I was finding it hard to tolerate. Noisy rooms, people clamoring about around me, or sometimes nothing at all set it off.

He gets it, I thought. *He hears me*. I imagined him reaching through that ruptured Plexiglas wall and taking hold of my hand. Finally, I was able to feel his touch.

Twelve

Wednesday, one week post-op, I got the green light to shower and wash my hair. It was cause enough for rejoicing. I had sponge bathed more than once, but my short hair still stood up in stiff smelly spikes. I couldn't shower myself, though. My feet were numb and my legs wobbled when I tried to stand. I could not keep my balance. And besides, the slightest exertion wore me out. I had been counting on Debbie to help me. She was, after all, a nurse, and the thought of someone else's inexperienced fingers shampooing my tender skull made me squeamish. What if the wound opened up?

Debbie sat me in the shower on a green plastic lawn chair retrieved from the basement. I was able to wash my upper body, and Debbie ran a soft washcloth over my back and legs. She picked through my scalp with care, separating strands of hair from clots of blood and the jelly-like goop leftover from the EEG.

"Okay, that's it. You're done," Debbie said, steadying the chair and helping me up. I wrapped a bath towel around me and then slipped into a thick white terry robe, a souvenir of my first trip to Europe years ago. With timid fingers, I ran a comb through my hair. I felt almost human again. Only the six inches of incision, rough and bumpy, remained as a reminder of my likeness to Frankenstein's monster.

"Over here," Debbie said patting the edge of the bed. I sat down and closed my eyes while she blow-dried my hair. I was so grateful to her for this wash and dry, her final act of kindness before she returned to Boston that afternoon. Smelling like lavender, I slipped under the covers and fell into a deep sleep.

    The next morning the pain alarm sounded at 5 a.m. I peeled back the covers so as not to wake Andy and, leaning into my walker, maneuvered out of bed. I shuffled first to the bathroom and then down the hallway to the kitchen. My head throbbed. Though extra-strength Tylenol brought relief, it did so at the price of an upset stomach. Percocet became my drug of choice.

    My stomach growled. I nuked some water for tea, grabbed a jar of peanut butter and a box of crackers, and placed both on the wicker cart we kept in the kitchen. I let go of my walker, leaned into the cart, and pushed it the ten feet into the dining room. Legs trembling from the effort, I sank into the chair and remained there for the next two hours. I was too exhausted to move anywhere more comfortable. Preparation of this little snack had cost me more energy than I could spare. As the Percocet worked its magic the pain receded, and I grew mellow and contemplative. I wondered what lessons were yet to be learned now that the tumor was gone. Soon, though, even the wondering ceased as an abiding quiet washed over me and I grew very still. The stillness reminded me of the intermittent experiences that began last summer—the ones about which I had been both curious and dismissive.

    The first time the stillness had descended the past June, I had settled into an orchestra seat on our patio to view the ballet of butterflies dancing over a Buddleia bush, thick with spikes of purple blossoms. The sky was a robin's egg blue. Sunlight bounced off leaves in a dozen shades of green. I was mesmerized by the colors of the day. While the butterflies fluttered and the goldfinches twittered, I sank into stillness. I was aware of the rise and fall of my breath, and my inability to move my limbs. Time seemed to stop. There was no past or future, only an eternal present. I was not afraid; I was both serene and joyful. I had had similar experiences many years

My Father the Fish

earlier, and they were gifts I treasured. Then, as now, when movement returned and life's clock began to tick again, I was disappointed, not relieved.

In my early twenties, I had been hiking with my boyfriend on Bear Mountain. While he was fussing with his camera lens, I continued on down the trail. At some point, I veered off onto a deer path to see what lay in that direction. I came to the edge of the mountain and looked out over a valley on fire with peak fall foliage. It was unspeakably beautiful. I sat myself down, legs dangling over the rocky rim, and watched the migrating hawks riding the thermals. They soared across a backdrop of bluest blue, and I was transfixed, motionless.

I have often heard people say, "I lost track of the time," but that is not what happened to me. I didn't lose track of it, I lost it altogether. I was gone for so long that my boyfriend, unable to find me, grew worried and alerted the park ranger who initiated a search. It was my name on the wind that ultimately brought me to my feet. I followed the path back to the trail and headed in the direction of the voices. All were relieved to find me unhurt, and I was confused. What was all the fuss about? I was sure it could have been no more than a handful of minutes since I had left my boyfriend to his picture taking and walked on ahead. But, he informed me (with no small measure of consternation), it had been close to an hour. For him maybe, but not for me. While I sat on the rim of the mountain, time had not passed at all.

Not too many years later, time had stopped again. On Friday nights in the ashram we would assemble crossed legged on our pillows in the temple for satsang, a gathering in which Gurudev would discourse on the Work. Sometimes he spoke on a topic of his choosing. More often he responded to our questions. That night the energy in the room was palpable. I felt as though his words were being directed to me alone. When our eyes met I had the sensation of being lifted, not simply off my pillow, but out of my body, into an infinite spaciousness that existed outside of linear time. The experience lasted for a couple of hours, long after satsang had ended and everyone else had left the temple. I had sat unmoving, desiring nothing, content to just BE.

Was it any wonder then that over the past summer I had cherished each experience of stillness in which time dissolved and took on a quality of endless space? Was it any wonder that I never thought to consider the experience a symptom of a brain gone awry?

The quiet dreaminess brought on by the Percocet had called up the memories of timelessness, but those incidents themselves had nothing in common with the state induced by the narcotic. When I relaxed into the effect of the drug, the resultant mental state was one of unfocused wooziness. During the handful of moments when I had been cocooned in a profound interruption to the forward march of time, I was hyper-alert, super-aware. I perceived a world that was far richer than my everyday reality. Colors were vibrant, electric, alive. Edges were sharp. Sounds were clear and distinct one from the other. Yet even with all this sensory distinction, there was an overriding unity, an all-oneness. I did not feel like an outside observer, but rather an integral part of all I observed. I tasted what it meant to be wholly absent of fear. Unfortunately, this broader awareness never lasted. Once the press of time exerted itself, I re-entered a reality shaped by my narrowness and my fears. Still, these accidental breakthroughs (into what, higher consciousness?) were for me incontrovertible proof of what the Work had taught me. There was a reality beyond my day-to-day experience, and I had the potential to enter into it and to make that reality mine.

Andy has a daughter, Reva. She was twenty-six at the

time of my surgery, but fifteen when I first met her. Andy and I were living in Chattanooga at the time, and Reva lived with her mother on a horse farm in rural Virginia. Andy was seeing very little of Reva in those days. He had told me he saw her with greater regularity when she was younger, but as she entered her teens, spending time with her dad ranked lower on her priority list than time with her friends and her horses. Her mother hadn't helped. She had run interference in Reva's relationship with her dad ever since they first separated. This was what Andy told me, but it hadn't taken long for me to see it for myself.

Since Andy and I had been married, we had seen Reva once, sometimes twice, a year. I didn't have much of a relationship with her. I had felt that she liked me from the start, but she wasn't my daughter. Never having had a child, I didn't quite know how to relate to one who showed up in my home a couple of times a year and never seemed too happy to be there. Andy adored Reva but, for the most part, she seemed indifferent towards him at best, rude and disrespectful at worst. I ached for him and was none too happy with this grown child, whose behavior too often wounded the love of my life.

Reva was never good about returning emails or phone calls. Back in December, after Andy told her about my diagnosis, she offered to come right away, but Andy told her that it would be better if she waited until after the surgery. He didn't hear from her again for seven weeks. When they finally did connect Reva chatted about her job and her horses but never asked how I was doing. After the call, Andy sat and cried, and I found myself struggling to have at least as much compassion for this child as I had for my husband.

It came as a great surprise to me when, a few days before the surgery, Reva phoned to say she wanted to come up to help out when I got home from the hospital. Andy was thrilled, and I looked forward to seeing her The previous summer she had traveled with us in Israel and France. It was

161

the first time I'd ever spent more than a few days with her. For me, something had changed on that trip. She seemed more open to me, more genuine, and I felt we had bonded—at least a little. Maybe there was a place for me in her life and for her in mine. I hoped one day we three could feel like a family.

Reva arrived and Debbie returned home, a changing of the guard. Reva has her dad's eyes and dark wavy hair, but not his build. She is a tall woman with broad shoulders, and an ample and curvaceous figure. Her muscular arms and back befit one who has been hauling hay for horses since she was a little girl. Now, she rolled up her sleeves and pitched right in helping wherever help was needed. Andy's mood shifted; where he had been my somber but optimistic companion—now he was buoyant. I knew having Reva with us was a shot in the arm for him. It was for me, as well.

Reva helped me dress and get ready for my Friday checkup with Dr. Piepmeier at Yale New Haven's outpatient facility, Temple Medical Center, a large multistory building in downtown New Haven. I told Reva there was no need for her to come with us. She was due some alone time.

It was only a twenty-minute ride to the medical center, and Andy parked in the adjoining garage. There was an elevator right there that took us up to Dr. Piepmeier's floor. The door opened to a large waiting area lined with rows and rows of plastic chairs. Some people were in wheelchairs. Some of the women were bald, and many had swathed their heads in colorful scarves. The sign over the desk indicated what I had already figured out. This was a waiting area for cancer patients. Chemotherapy was right down the hall.

Benign, I reminded myself. The meningioma was benign, it was out, and I was fine. Still, I jerked upright the moment my name was called. I couldn't get myself out of there fast enough. But I wasn't fast. I was slow—taking my small, measured steps behind my walker. A nurse showed us into a compact, no-frills examination room. I sat down on the exam

My Father the Fish

table. Andy took the only chair. In minutes Dr. Piepmeier strode in with Betsy, the one I had called Nurse Lady, and a couple of fourth-year medical students. Being treated at a teaching hospital, I had learned to always expect a crowd. Andy and I were introduced to the two white-coated young men.

"You look great," Dr. Piepmeier said. "How do you feel?"

I told him about the balance issues, the wonging, and the ear ringing while he ran me through a brief neurological exam.

"Take a walk," he said placing the walker at the other end of the room. "Don't worry. We won't let you fall." The two young white coats took up positions on either side of me. I stood up and with great concentration stepped forward. One more step and then I wavered into the arms of white coat number one.

"Ok. Sit down," Dr. Piepmeier said. "In another week you won't need that walker. You're doing great. Really great."

My face lit up like a third grader who had just received a gold star on her spelling test. If I had to be a patient, I at least wanted to be the best patient.

"You're healing well. Staples are ready to come out," he said. Pluck. Pluck. Pluck. Each tug pinched at my scalp and I winced. Although Andy had told me they had stapled my skull together, I had never truly embraced the idea. Instead, I had continued to picture coarse black thread whip-stitching my head together. Yet there they were, the staples, lying at the bottom of a metal dish looking like the ones the installer had used to tack the bedroom carpet in place. I got woozy.

I left the exam room in a volley of good cheer. Everyone was truly happy at how well I was doing, especially me. We had one more stop before heading home. I had gotten a call from Lorna Multy in the Patient Relations Office of the hospital. She wanted to meet with me. Although I had not issued any kind of formal complaint after my experience with Dr. Gardiner, the hospital apparently had a protocol for addressing patient dissatisfaction. Dr. Vives reported what I had told him to the chief of neurology who had called me at home a couple of days after the incident. He offered a profuse apology on behalf of Dr. Gardiner and the entire hospital.

Ms. Multy was waiting for me when I came out of the examination room. She ushered me to an empty office where we could talk. She wanted me to recount the episode with Dr. Gardiner. I didn't need another apology. I also wasn't looking to get Dr. Gardiner in trouble. I never thought he meant to scare the pants off me. He was, I believed, full of himself and perhaps a little too much of the eager beaver. He had rushed to share test results with me like a political analyst announcing the winner before the polls had closed. What I wanted to see was a change in the way these doctors were trained in patient relations and communications.

"I could help," I told her, "by speaking to residents and med school students about what it's like to be on the receiving end of their words." This was something I really wanted to do. I was a good speaker and I understood the problem. If I shared my experience maybe I could make a difference; maybe I could save some other patients from a similar occurrence of terrifying miscommunication.

Ms. Multy said it was a wonderful idea. "We recently formed a Patient Advisory Board," she said. "Maybe you could be on that. Let me think this through and see where you could fit, and I'll get back to you."

But she never did. I didn't lose my enthusiasm for the project, but my energy was so low for so long, I didn't follow through with her either. I still want to do it someday. It was a way I could honor Gurudev, Mataji, and their commitment to bringing the principles of holistic health into the mainstream through traditional educational channels. Many people, it seemed, were confused about holistic health. I often heard people equate the term with everything from homeopathy to reiki. Holistic health was not a modality but an approach to sickness and well-being. Did the doctor see only an ailing body part that needed repair like a faulty carburetor, or did he see the whole person?

I exited through the doors of Temple Medical Center feeling energized and optimistic about my future. At home, though, I crawled into bed. The energy generated by the visits only went so far. It had been a big day with more energy expended than I had in my storehouse; another round of wonging set in. When I woke it was already Shabbat. Reva and Andy had prepared a sumptuous meal of green salad, roast chicken with rosemary potatoes, challah, and wine, and I was determined to sit at the table and enjoy it with them.

After dinner, Reva offered to help me with a shower before she returned home to Ohio the following morning. I still needed help and was appreciative. She stacked towels and a washcloth and lined up the shampoo and conditioner bottles in easy reach. Then she called me to come in to the bathroom. I felt unexpectedly shy. This was Reva, not my daughter nor my friend, and I felt self-conscious and vulnerable exposing my middle-aged body with its sags and blotchy imperfections.

I turned my back to Reva as I slipped my arms out of my robe and pressed it to my chest. Reva steadied the shower chair and helped me sit down.

"Ready?" she asked

"Ready."

Reva tilted her head, motioned toward my robe, and raised her eyebrows.

"Oh. Right," I said, handing her the robe. I soaped up with a washcloth under a trickle of water and lathered up my hair, then Reva washed my back and rinsed me down. She had the expert hands of someone who had bathed countless dogs and horses. Her touch was matter-of-fact, not tender, but it was also confident, and I relaxed into her competent hands. The intimacy of this encounter with Reva opened a door in my heart. After so many years, I trusted her enough to let her in, but I had no idea how or whether this deeper level of familiarity had affected Reva. Outwardly warm and convivial, she was not one to share her feelings. She was very hard to read, and still is.

♦♦♦

My balance improved with every day. As long as my fingertips were in contact with the wall I could keep my balance. My left foot felt almost normal. Only my right leg was still numb below the calf. I had started seeing a physical therapist a few days after I returned home. My first session was disheartening. I was unnerved by what I couldn't do—the simplest exercises and movements. The therapist was unfazed. "To be expected," he had told me and sent me home with an exercise regimen and twice weekly appointments for the next six weeks. I exercised twice daily without fail and proved wrong his prediction it would take six months for me to be walking on my own.

My days fell into a comfortable rhythm. I dressed and straightened the linens, but spent most of the day sitting up in bed. I still felt fragile. My bedroom was a safe cocoon. I meditated, journaled, kept up on my PT exercises, and continued to use visualization as a healing tool. Now that the brain tumor had kept its side of the bargain—released itself into Dr. Piepmeier's hands—I reframed my visualization with new images of healing:

I am muscled, naked, and tanned standing again on the beach at Keawakapu. The tide is out. Far in the distance I see my father the fish swimming towards me. He brings the ocean with him, and soon I am neck deep. I take a deep breath, hold it, and dunk beneath the water. Bobbing to the surface, I recite a traditional woman's prayer: "Blessed are You Lord our God who has commanded me to immerse in the

My Father the Fish

mikveh." I turn to the east and dunk again, then to the north, the west and south. With each submersion I imagine washing away any impurity of spirit that might impede my healing. Then, the ritual completed, I thank my father the fish for bringing these healing waters to me. I kiss his fish mouth, hold his fish gaze, and then say good-bye. He swims out toward the horizon taking the tide with him and I am left standing on dry sand, basking in the warmth of the sun.

Mikveh, Hebrew for a confluence of waters, is a ritual bath constructed to the exacting specifications delineated in the Talmud. It is also any natural body of water—an ocean, a river, a spring-fed lake. Unlike a bathhouse, a mikveh plays no role at all in physical hygiene. Immersion in the waters of the mikveh is said to elevate one to a status of holiness by conferring a spiritual state of purity. It is customary for a bride and groom to immerse in the mikveh before the wedding and for women to immerse monthly after menstruation. Mikveh is part of the conversion ritual and many men immerse before the Sabbath and especially before Yom Kippur, the Day of Atonement. An evolving modern custom incorporates mikveh in a healing ritual pre- or postsurgery or cancer treatment. At the time that I wove mikveh into my healing visualization I was unaware of this new practice. I very much believed there had been a psychic or emotional component behind the physical manifestation of my tumor, and so the idea of a ritual of spiritual purification felt natural to me.

Before my marriage to Andy ten years earlier, I had gone to a mikveh because it was important to him we have an orthodox Jewish wedding. The ritual of mikveh was a requirement. I had not been comfortable with the idea, which I had then viewed as primitive, superstitious nonsense. But it was easy enough to do and while it meant nothing to me it was significant to him. So I had gone along.

167

The mikveh at Andy's shul was a square, tiled pool filled chest-high with water. The room was clean and unadorned, the water crystal clear and chlorinated. The *rebbetzin*, rabbi's wife, was there to guide me through the process. She held a towel up in front of me and turned her eyes away as I disrobed, which only slightly minimized my feelings of awkwardness. I slipped into the chilly water, said the blessing as she instructed, and dunked myself expecting nothing more noteworthy than goose bumps, but I emerged thunderstruck.

"*Kasher, Kasher*," said the rebbetzin, indicating I had performed the rite according to custom and could climb out and dress.

But, I wasn't ready. I asked her if I could spend a few minutes alone in the pool.

"Take as long as you need," she said and left the room.

I submerged again and again, soaking up the energy of water that seemed to be vibrating. I felt elevated and purified in some way I could not begin to describe. There had been a palpable difference to this water just as I had experienced a profound and palpable difference in the air I breathed in the ashram's temple.

That pre-wedding experience of what was my first, but not my last, dunk in a mikveh, made an indelible impression on me. It was why I came up with the idea of visualizing myself submerged in a natural mikveh of ocean waters as a rite of healing. I felt I needed something more than surgery to exorcise the tumor. Perhaps immersing for real would have been a more effective ritual of spiritual purification, but it was winter, and I was not prepared to dunk my freshly reassembled skull into New Haven's community mikveh, healing energy or not.

I was always a big reader, but now keeping my eyes focused on a page for more than a short time proved difficult, and concentrating on anything for long exhausted me. Mike, my physical therapist, had told me to think of the brain as a muscle. Thinking, focusing, and paying attention all worked the muscle, he said. And since this muscle was in the process of healing, it needed to rest. That made sense to me and helped me to relax into relaxing. During those early days at home nothing beat being read to by Barbara Kingsolver, author of *Prodigal Summer*. Andy took the audio book out of the library for me. I gingerly set the headset on my crown, pushed play and waited. Kingsolver's voice, soothing as a cup of cocoa, was my companion for many days, and I meted out her reading in short increments lest the story and her company come to an end too soon.

I dozed, too, and gazed out the window content to watch the swaying of branches and shift of clouds through the winter sky. Time was fluid, and I flowed with it from one diversion to another as the mood moved me. Day advanced into night, night into day. I slept when tired, ate when hungry—following the beat of my internal rhythm. When, at six weeks post-op, I had complained to Dr. Piepmeier about how tired I was and how long it was taking to heal, he had simply said, "Be at peace with that." He was a man of few words, but he chose them well and for me they were the best medicine.

I spent hours sitting and thinking about the habitual patterns of thought, feeling, and behavior that ran interference as I tried to find some lasting peace. I thought a lot about fear. I was plagued by it, always had been. Much of the fear was focused on sickness and death. The fear was endlessly malleable, attaching itself to whatever was handy. I was afraid for myself, *what if the tumor comes back*, and afraid for Andy, *what if his car skids off the road*. I didn't expect to be able to eradicate the fear. But I knew it was possible to loosen the hold it had on me by taking a step back and watching the terrified Lorri as one might watch a character in a film. That is to say, with some distance and a measure of dispassion. I could recall an unafraid version of Lorri, and I could distinguish the present fear that grabbed Lorri by the throat, from the unchanging Self. I could know the fear as just a feeling, like a hot flash or a cold chill that, in time, would pass, and it would cease to overwhelm me.

Fear was not my only bugaboo. A whole range of thoughts and feelings had the power to take up all the space in the room if I let them. I held the intention of approaching all my experiences—my scattered thoughts, my feelings—as passing, and therefore, uncomfortable maybe, painful maybe, but not significant. What was significant was the Self that experienced. It was immutable, unlike the rotating cast of my one-woman show. I struggled every day to keep my feet planted on bedrock, not shifting sands.

Years ago, I had accepted *to know God* as one possible formulation of the answer to the question, What's the point? But what did that answer mean to me? My very notion of God was in flux, undulating between my idea of an Infinite Eternal Unqualified Reality and the God that was keeping an intimate and loving eye on me. Did God have to fit one schema or the other? Wasn't there plenty of room for both perspectives and a myriad more in between? Jewish texts speak of the seventy faces of Torah because while ultimately there is one Truth, that Truth looks different depending upon where you stand to view it. It is a matter of perspective, and perspective is a function of one's self-knowledge and understanding.

Who am I, really? If, as I believed, the Self was not other than God, then wasn't coming to know that Self apart from my experience—which included all my perceptions, thoughts and feelings—a way to better understand the nature of God? Could I come to know God by knowing the Self? Or, put another way, would it even be possible to ever know God if I didn't first come to know the Self?

Thirteen

During the months awaiting surgery and then recovering from it my energy was limited, and I had to dial back my activity level. I would wash a dish or two and straighten the bed, but had been relieved of my usual household duties of cleaning, cooking, and doing the laundry. Those I left for Andy. Out of necessity my priorities were shifting. I was learning to not sweat the small stuff and I was discovering life could go on with the bed unmade and dishes in the sink. I was learning to, as Dr. Piepmeier had instructed, *be at peace with that*, and so much more. The pace of my life had slowed dramatically, and I was choosing to spend much of my time in stillness: reading, reflecting, pondering, praying. My mind quieted, freeing up energy previously consumed by endless inner chatter and anxiety.

Often when I sat alone doing nothing more than watching the dance of the maple leaves or the to and fro of a robin constructing its nest, I was reminded of what it was like living in Israel without a car. I walked everywhere: in the *wadi*, down goat and camel trails through short stretches of desert, climbing out again closer to the center of town where I followed the road to the supermarket or post office or bank. I loved the walks then, but appreciated them ever so much more after we returned to the States. Back in Connecticut, I would hop into my car, navigate the ten minutes to the grocery store, jump out, wind my way through the aisles avoiding the end-cap displays and carts of other shoppers, and then hop back into the car for the stop and go trip home. I missed the solitude of the walks in Israel, and the stretch of time that separated me from my destination—time in which my mind would open like a flower. There I had found a space in which I could reflect and settle more deeply into myself. As much as I had valued that experience, I had let it slip away when I left the desert and its wadis behind. I saw I had an opportunity now to do my life differently.

I was tasting what it was like to grow old. In his book, *From Aging to Sage-ing*, Reb Zalman wrote that at some point in their elder years most people found they had neither the energy nor inclination to be engaged in the world in the same ways they once were. The dimming of both eyesight and hearing, together with diminished energy made it more difficult to engage. Reb Zalman suggested the confluence of these physical losses was no accident. It was the work of the Divine creating conditions well suited to introspection, meditation and prayer. "God was in search of man," said the mystic and theologian Abraham Joshua Heschel. He desired relationship. Perhaps the losses that came with aging were God's attempt to create the conditions that could draw us closer. If that were so, then maybe my current limitations were the work of God helping me to draw close too.

The first week or so, I was never alone. While Debbie or Reva were around, Andy went to his office. After they left, he worked from home. It was apparent that if Andy was to return full-time to his job, which provided our income and only health insurance, we required help. I needed rides to physical therapy and to doctor appointments, and we needed dinner prepared so I could eat at a normal hour and not have to wait until Andy got home to put together a meal. I didn't have a network of friends to call upon and my family was not nearby. I felt isolated, yet had faith help would come. And it did—from the most unlikely places.

While we were still considering our options, Rabbi Haston, a local Chabad rabbi, rallied his contacts in the community to come to our aid. So many women responded to the rabbi's request that in short order my freezer was packed, and a name and phone number were scrawled on my calendar next to each of my PT appointments. It was quite remarkable. Women I knew only casually, as well as women I'd never even met, began arriving at my door with meals: herb-roasted chicken, soup with fluffy matzo balls, and string beans almondine; whole wheat lasagna, tossed mesclun salad, and garlic bread. Andy and I ate very well. There were always leftovers for me to heat up for my lunch, and the donated meals cut down on the number of trips Andy had to make to the grocery store. These women's generosity with their time allowed Andy to pursue his career and keep bringing home a paycheck.

The first few weeks post-op, while I was still pretty weak and dealing with pain, it was easier to accept help. But as I grew stronger, I became more and more uncomfortable with all the taking. I didn't like the way accepting help served to underscore the fact that my life was not as it used to be. Sometimes the very act of popping one of those lovingly prepared meals into the oven made me feel like an invalid, and I couldn't stand that.

So when Rabbi Haston called and said, "There's this woman Sara. You don't know her, but she'd like to help you out. What do you need?" I was glad to be able to tell him I really didn't need anything. My freezer was full. I had rides to all my appointments.

"Are you sure?" Rabbi asked. "Maybe there's something?"

"Yes, quite sure," I said, a little irked by his persistence.

"Well, the thing is, she just retired and is feeling a bit at a loss. She wants to do something meaningful with her time. Isn't there anything she could do for you?"

That really annoyed me. I was the one recovering from brain surgery. Was it my problem this woman (whom I didn't even know) was having an identity crisis now that her job no longer defined her!

Wow! What a bitch I am, I thought. I'd spent a lot of time with my attitudes under the microscope and I had few illusions. Compassion was not my strong suit. My go-to position was more often selfish and guarded than generous of spirit, and here was but another case in point. Thank god the Watcher was watching; and under her piercing gaze, the Bitch slunk off the stage.

It was not a big stretch for me to take a walk in Sara's shoes. I was struggling everyday to be okay with this version of myself who couldn't do any of the things that in the past gave me a sense of accomplishment. How did I feel now that I wasn't working? Not great. Sometimes I remembered who I am is not a function of what I do, but is a spark of God, the Eternal, Unchanging. But then there were other moments when the absence of a paycheck left me feeling inadequate, and I would look to Andy to reassure me that it didn't matter, that he still loved me.

The essence of the Work is coming to realize one's nothingness, or no-thing-ness, for I am not a thing. The Kabbalists expressed the same idea but from the opposite direction. They aspired toward *bitul hayesh*, the nullification of one's somethingness, what Freud called the ego. Remembering my true nature and letting go of my self-valuing was an ongoing struggle. Yes, I had more than an inkling of an idea of what Sara might be going through.

"Know what?" I said to Rabbi Haston. "Maybe she can come and help me make a salad. I'd really like to do some meal prep for myself but I can't stand very long. She could help me wash and cut up the vegetables."

The rabbi was more than delighted, maybe grateful. He said he would arrange it.

The following afternoon Sara showed up. She was around my age, maybe a few years older, with mousy brown hair and a full figure. She was dressed casually in snug fitting pants and a pullover sweater. She didn't look familiar. She was pleasant enough and very talkative. Seeing Tova asleep on the doggie bed, Sara launched into one story after another about the escapades of her own pooches. Together we peeled and chopped cucumber and carrot and washed and spun lettuce and baby greens. I don't think we were together more than two hours, but when she left she was bubbling with enthusiasm and good spirit.

I was left thinking about giving and receiving. These two actions, usually set in juxtaposition, were not opposites. They were two halves of a whole. From one perspective I was the one in need, Sara the one who was there to give. From another, our roles were reversed. I provided the opportunity for her to be of use and feel worthwhile. We were both givers and receivers. I had been so self-absorbed in not wanting to be perceived as needy, I had not considered that providing an opportunity to give was also a kindness. I hadn't considered *other* at all. My afternoon with Sara shook me up and out of my self-indulgence. Somewhere along the way my commitment to self-care had become tainted by self-involvement. After my encounter with Sara I began expecting less and offering more, even when all I could offer was gratitude.

Low energy wasn't the only factor keeping me from engaging life in the way I had before. The wonging I had described to Andy when I first returned home after surgery had continued. Bright lights and loud noises, even background music brought it on. I could not sit in a crowded restaurant. The competing conversations and the clank of silverware were intolerable. The flicker of light on a television or monitor screen drove me batty. Sometimes bending over was enough to set off the temple gong. No one I spoke to could make sense of what I meant by wonging. It wasn't until several years later that I met a woman who knew exactly what I meant. She also had a brain tumor. She listened to my description of wonging, wide-eyed. "I know," she whispered, and I cried to finally have been understood. None of my doctors (or hers) could explain the wonging. Dr. Piepmeier said, "Be patient. The brain takes time to heal."

On top of this I had ringing in my left ear. All the time. I had made peace with a level of interior background noise that would fade in and out of my awareness like the hum of fluorescent lighting tended to do. But sometimes the sound would escalate to a high-pitched whine that curdled my spinal fluid like the sound of chalk screeching on a blackboard always did. Other times the din inside my head became so loud it was hard for me to hear the sounds around me... Andy's voice, a chirping bird, a car driving by. It kept me awake many nights. I was overtired and cranky.

The ringing had started before surgery, right after I began taking the Keppra to prevent seizures. I was convinced the drug was responsible. In a follow-up visit with Dr. Piepmeier I brought up my theory. He promised me the drug could not have caused the ringing. I wasn't surprised. At a visit some weeks before I had reported to him that since I'd been taking Keppra I wasn't having hot flashes or being awakened by night sweats.

"This pill is ideal for women going through menopause," I said. "How's that for an off-label indication!"

His lips had curled into the most tentative of smiles, but he shook his head. As with the ear ringing, my experience didn't seem to count for anything. He wanted me to stay on the Keppra for a full year to be sure there would be no more seizures. I remained convinced there was some causative connection between the drug and the ringing. Anyway, staying on the Keppra for a year didn't make any sense to me. The tumor caused the seizures. The tumor was gone. The swelling had gone down. Why would I still need antiseizure meds? But Dr. Piepmeier said this was protocol. He assured me that in his experience.... blah, blah, blah. I was not persuaded, and we began to bargain.

"Three months," I said, figuring I was already one third of the way there.

"Six months," he countered. "If you are seizure-free."

I agreed. It was better than a year, and I was too afraid of having another seizure to disregard his advice altogether even with the ear ringing and the continued fatigue, which he did attribute to the Keppra.

He suggested I see an ENT, ear nose and throat specialist, which I did. The ENT didn't think the Keppra was causing the ringing either. What I had was tinnitus. There were many possible causes, he explained. One being brain tumor or injury, another being exposure to a deafening blast. This last caught my attention. What could be more deafening than the explosion in my psyche that followed Dr. Gardiner's pronouncement of a possibly fatal brain tumor? I was no stranger to the mind-body relationship and the havoc that stress could wreak. If, I postulated, the threat of a fatal diagnosis had caused it, I wondered if the ringing would stop once I came to terms with the inevitability of my own death.

I was quite practiced at acknowledging with absolute certainty that all biological life comes to an end. Yet, that acknowledgment and even my own faith in the immortality of the Self did little to quell the terror I felt when entertaining thoughts of my own death. I didn't think I could ever find peace without first coming to a real and lasting acceptance of death, together with all it implied. Bliss, I supposed, might be the experience resulting from an equanimous relationship with death.

Sometimes I thought the reason I had a brain tumor was to force this very issue. When I looked at it that way, I saw the meningioma as a gift. The most significant consequence of staring my own physical mortality in the eye was that I had a fire lit under me and this intensified my resolve to do the Work. Now. In this moment. I did not have all the time in the world. I never had.

The specialist offered little hope the ringing would ever go away.

"Just learn to live with it," he said.

The best he could suggest was I try to block out the ringing by listening to recordings of white sound or whale calls or torrents of water rushing through the rainforest. I left his office in a funk, overwhelmed by the possibility of the ringing being permanent. I thought of my father and all his one-day-at-a-time wisdom. Just for today, he would surely tell me, live with it.

Later that week, Andy and I were taking a walk in the early evening. We paused to rest by a small pond in a fen. A chorus of tree frogs and crickets serenaded us.
"It stopped!" I said.
"What stopped?"
"The ringing!"
Peace at last, although the ringing hadn't actually stopped. Nature's chorale had drowned it out. When I paid close attention I could still hear it. Later that evening Andy returned to the fen with a tape recorder and made a cassette for me. I played it every evening when I went to bed, falling asleep to the chirps and clicks.

Tree frogs and crickets could get me through the night, but what about all day? Walking around with a headset and recorder was a possibility but not a practical one. I needed a better strategy for dealing with the ringing, and I came up with one. The next time it got very loud I went into my room, sat down, closed my eyes and focused my attention on the ringing itself. Rather than turn away from it, I dove right into the middle of the din and watched, or I should say, *listened*. When I silently shouted, "I can't stand this anymore!" and I wanted to run, I watched that too from a place of detached interest. Each time I cringed at a loud blast, I located the site of tension and released it, gently massaging the muscles with my mind. I began to float in the sound and to explore it.

The novel, *Blood Music*, told the story of a single alien life form that spread across the Earth incorporating into itself all living things—people, animals, plants—until all life became part of it; The One. The alien's blood, coursing through its circulatory system, sounded the notes of all the life it had absorbed. I imagined the ringing in my ears to be a chorus like this blood music, singing the song of my own life, the one I was so grateful to still call my own. Each time the ringing became unbearable I would think of blood music and relax into the sound until it subsided.

♦♦♦

As my energy and endurance returned it became harder and harder to turn my attention inward. I fidgeted. I paced. I wanted to get busy and do things—anything, little things, so long as they made me feel my life was getting back to normal. And what was normal: busyness, activity, a to-do list with all the entries ticked off? I felt pressured to return to the communal rhythm: sleep at night, rise in the morning, work on weekdays. The pressure was not coming from Andy. It was coming from myself. Everyone else was still in the "Lorri is healing" mode. No one was expecting any more of me than I felt ready and able to do, but I had always been a compulsive task-doer relishing the moment I could check off completed items on my to-do list. It would take more than a brain tumor to erase that pattern. I knew I needed to face my attitudes and confront my values head on in order to change. Managing the internal pressure I felt would help as well, and my friend Rosalie gave me an idea.

I took out index cards and two blank envelopes. On the face of one envelope I wrote, *Options to be Dealt with Later: when I'm healed, and ready*. On the other I wrote, *Taking care of Lorri: Options for Today*. Then, I began to list the various tasks I was pressuring myself to complete, one item to a card. In the coming weeks, my stack of cards grew as more "I shoulds" presented themselves. They ran the gamut:
  —Work in garden
  —Label photos and put in albums

—Clean out file drawers in den and basement
—Take care of my spiritual self: visualization, meditate, journal, pray
—Take care of my physical self: rest, yoga, tai chi, walk
—Write poetry
—Organize *Sage-ing Curriculum Resource Guide*
—Follow up: speaking to Yale medical residents

Each morning, I reviewed the entries on the cards and decided which I might deal with that day. Those I placed in the envelope labeled *Options for Today*. The rest of the cards I tucked inside the envelope labeled *Options to be Dealt with Later*. Referring to each "I should" as an option as opposed to a mandatory task, helped to remind me of the bigger picture—not one index card listed an item whose doing or not doing on any particular day would in and of itself make one wit of difference in my life. All along, I could hear my mother asking me the question I heard from her often as a stressed-out child and teenager. "How important is it?" she would say about the math test I was fretting over or the pimple on my chin. "Years from now, do you think you will even remember this?" Her wise perspective got me through tough times back then and was helping me again.

On a milder day, one that hinted at the coming of spring, I ventured down the driveway to pick up our mail. Each piece of correspondence I pulled from the box reminded me, in its own way, of how much I had to be grateful for. The first envelope contained an invoice from the company that had supplied the walker I no longer needed to rely upon. The second, a bright pink envelope with a Redwood Forest postal stamp, held a get-well card signed by several of my sage-ing colleagues. I only recognized one of the names. They wrote, "Sending you reiki energy for your healing," and I was reminded of how many people had sent and continued to send me their prayers and best wishes. A standard white number 10 envelope contained a letter from Yale New Haven Hospital requesting my participation in a study aimed at determining why some people developed brain lesions and others didn't. Was there a genetic factor? I would participate because it was a way for me to give back, to express my gratitude for the care I had received. It was a way to pay it forward. The last piece in the mailbox was a Miller Nurseries Spring Catalog. I saw in its glossy pages ablaze with photos of annuals, perennials, flowering shrubs, and vegetables, a promise for the future. I would continue to grow and bear fruit.

♦♦♦

By all accounts I was healing rapidly, though the path to wellness was not following a straight-line trajectory. After a few very good days, a bad one would send the reality of how far I still had to go smashing into the hope that I was there already. Still, overall, the headaches were less frequent, I was sleeping better, and I was able to read for short stints. I was getting stronger, though some days even a load of laundry or a sink of dirty dishes was more than I could handle. My ear still rang but I was learning to live with it. It was the wonging that carved out the great divide between recovering and recovered. The all-too-frequent episodes of temple gongs reverberating in my skull kept me from fully re-entering life as I had lived it before the surgery. But then again, was that what I even wanted?

I had been working with LycoRed Ltd. as a regulatory consultant and writer for eight years. I made my own hours and I worked from home. The work had been steady and took up a good chunk of each week. My plan had been to diminish my involvement with LycoRed projects as I developed a steady stream of clients for my sage-ing programs, little by little shifting my income to another source rather than reducing it.

"Andy," I said one night as we sat together propped up in bed. "What would you think if I didn't go back to working for LycoRed? I mean, I know I'm not ready to anyway, but what if when I was… I didn't?"

Andy didn't respond, but I could see he was listening.

"You know that saying about taking the hardships of life and rendering them spiritual?" I asked. "Well, I've been thinking. What if I write a book describing how I've been using this whole experience of the brain tumor as fodder for my own growth? I think it would be a good way to consolidate what I've learned so I don't lose it."

"A book's a good idea," he said.

I waited, hoping for more, then continued.

"I want to be able to take care of the house and help in the garden, but my energy level fluctuates day to day and I only have so much left over for other things. I still need to move at my own pace. Meeting project deadlines for LycoRed feels like more than I can handle right now, and I do still want to promote my sage-ing programs… but not yet. I can't do everything, and I want to make sure that I don't sacrifice what is of real importance for what is not."

Still, he was quiet.

"I'm talking about you being our sole support. And continuing to use some of our savings if we have to. Would you be okay with that?"

"It's been three months since you had a paycheck," he said. "And we've been managing so far. So, sure, if that's what you want to do, that's okay with me."

I was relieved, but not surprised. Savings are for a rainy day, and this brain tumor had been more than a drizzle. Besides, Andy didn't need much. Give him a bowl of soup, a home-grown tomato, and a grass hut, and he was happy. And he was practical. If we could get by on his salary alone, that was fine with him.

The only remaining problem was me, or to be more

accurate that me who took every paycheck as an affirmation of my worth. She would not be okay without a job title and a significant income. She would take her old life back in a heartbeat, as soon as physically able to do so, and she would justify why it was the only reasonable thing to do.

I knew her and all my cast members well. That was a saving grace. I knew what to expect. Like mischievous children, one by one, they scampered across my life's stage. As long as the Watcher in the balcony kept her eye on them, they couldn't wreak havoc. Observing the players, remembering the Self, and keeping my aim to know God in sharp focus sometimes felt like juggling a multitude of colored balls. It took work, an act of will, and constant redirecting of attention to keep them all in the air.

But what choice did I have? Time was short. I had tasted the truth of that firsthand when Dr. Gardiner laid out the possibility of aggressive cancer. I could not afford to keep investing energy in efforts that would not bear the fruit I most wanted to taste. The life I had been leading had veered off in the wrong direction. I began to envision a daily schedule that gave priority to time spent in direct support of my inner work. While uncritical self-observation was at the heart of the Work process, and it could and in fact should, take place in every moment irrespective of whether I was practicing tai chi, doing laundry, or paying bills, there was no doubt that my process would benefit from continuing to set time aside for meditation and reflection. My life had been quiet before, but in the future, I promised myself it would be quieter still.

♦♦♦

It was my desire for meaningful work that had set me on the path to sage-ing certification. I was driven by a desire to give back to Gurudev, and by a very strong and very right feeling that knowing God firsthand would require much more of me. In part, I blamed my spiritual floundering on what I was *doing*, in other words, on my day-to-day involvement with the business of doing business. However valuable my contribution to LycoRed had been, I knew, in the end, it was all meaningless trivia.

But, in fact, the nature of my job was never the problem.

An Indian holy woman with many children to feed was asked when she found the time to meditate.

"When I stir the soup," she said.

Just so, I didn't have to rally the troops to fight world hunger, teach conflict resolution in inner city schools, or sit in full lotus in a Himalayan cave to engage with a spiritual life. The Work had to be done whether I was supervising regulatory compliance, teaching principles of sage-ing, or tending flocks of chickens or disciples. It was an inner psychological process. No special circumstances were required. Meaning was inherent, not in the type of work, but only in what I brought to the work.

Still, my desire to devote myself to a field in which engaging with the principles of spiritual development was part and parcel of the job wasn't a mistake. It was sly. Given how easy it was to be swept along by the currents of life, creating a situation for myself that would stem the tide was not at all a bad idea. Using the sage-ing work to support my inner efforts to do the Work, was smart.

The problem was, once I had completed my training and focused on developing a viable sage-ing business, I (or to be accurate, a member of my cast), forgot that this new career direction was intended only as a means to a higher end. This cast member saw the potential for success, for kudos, for esteem, and it was she who sped along the highway that December night when the world went flat. She was the one who refused to pull off the road, who didn't notice her life was in danger of being extinguished. And while she pressed on to the meeting, the Watcher dozed in the balcony, and thus I failed to keep my eye on the real prize.

I had chosen to see the tumor as my teacher and that was a useful and calming image for me to hold onto. But, the tumor was not my teacher. It was only the catalyst. It brought my life to a grinding halt, pushed me up against the wall of my own mortality, and caused me to reassess what I was doing and why. It set off a shock wave that shattered complacency and reminded me of what I had all but forgotten—my aim and purpose in this life. I had been so focused on finding so-called meaningful work, I had lost sight of the fact that I had already found it years ago in *the Work*, and as long as I was engaged in the practice of it, it mattered not at all what my job was. I learned powerful lessons, but they were not spoon fed to me by a mythical teacher in the guise of a tumor. They were learned through my own efforts to apply the teachings I had received from Gurudev.

♦♦♦

Early in September I had my next checkup with Dr. Piepmeier. I took extra care picking out flattering slacks and a short-sleeved cotton sweater, fixing my short hair the best I could, and applying eye makeup I usually reserved for weddings and business meetings. I was invested in looking good and healthy. I had a case to make. I wanted to get off the Keppra, and he had promised at this visit he would re-evaluate the continuation of the medication. After a brief exam, my assurances that there had been no more seizures, and a discussion about how I was feeling, Dr. Piepmeier agreed I could stop taking the Keppra. I was flying when I left his office, ready to celebrate. *Now*, I thought, *I will get my life back*! Within a few drug-free days, my energy level began to increase, and the episodes of wonging decreased in frequency, although the ringing in my ear did not go away.

I was taking care of most of the basic household day to day tasks with only a little help. Although I had been given the okay to get behind the wheel again, I had no inclination to venture out much. I puttered in the garden. I read and I wrote. I sat on the patio warmed by the sun and thought about my life. I snoozed. I sought out quiet from within the confines of my own chatterbox mind. I no longer needed the community support I had relied upon in the first few months. Though I had said many thank yous, I wanted to do something more to acknowledge these folks who had helped in such a big way. Andy suggested we host a *seudah hoda'a*, a feast of thanksgiving.

Perfect, I said. *"I know who the guest of honor will be."*

Reb Zalman had taught me an exercise in gratitude he called a testimonial dinner to Life's severe teachers. He said it had been inspired by a verse from Psalm 23. "You prepare a table before me in the presence of my enemies." The exercise involved imagining a banquet at which the guest of honor was a severe teacher—a person who had in some way made your life very difficult. Perhaps it was a boss who fired you without cause, a lover who spurned you, or a banker who foreclosed on your house. As Master of Ceremonies you were expected to deliver the address outlining the perceived injustice that had been inflicted upon you by this severe teacher followed by the unexpected good that had resulted from the experience. The brain tumor was the severe teacher I intended to toast at my seudah hoda'a.

I began planning the celebration. I invited all my family and friends who had helped out in any way: Jean and Bill who cared for Tova on the day of surgery, Garrett who picked me up and brought me to the fitness room at Woodbridge Town Center, Joan and Harold who stepped up whenever asked, the many chefs who had catered my meals, and more. The weather cooperated. There was plenty of wine and beer and platters of food and a super-sized carrot cake from Claire's, a local vegetarian eatery.

We have a large, lush backyard with a flagstone patio and a screened-in porch. My guests filled every chair and some picnicked on blankets on the lawn. It was difficult for me to be in the midst of so much chatter, so I took breaks when I had to, pulling a chair off to the side, quietly soaking up the sunshine and the good spirits. When it looked like everyone had eaten and drunk their fill, Andy brought out the carrot cake with the words Thank You written in turquoise blue icing across the top. I drummed up the energy to make a short speech thanking everyone for all their love, help, and support before giving a nod of acknowledgment to the very special role the tumor had played in my life.

"Benign or not, a brain tumor is a brain tumor, and I wouldn't wish one on anyone," I said. "But all in all, it's hard for me to think about my experience as anything less than a blessing. I learned so much through the events and circumstances set in motion by the brain tumor. I was offered opportunities to grow that I might not have had otherwise. I learned how to pray from the heart to a God that could hear me, to visualize a positive outcome with hope and conviction, to embrace the reality that each day could well be my last."

I looked around at all the faces, some smiling, some serious, all attentive.

"I learned how to ask for help and accept it gracefully. And look what I got in return," I said with a sigh. "You guys. New friends. A place in community. Thank you all."

My two-minute speech left me high but depleted. I accepted a plate of carrot cake from Andy, retreated inside, and curled my legs up under me on the couch. My ear was ringing, my head was vibrating with a low level wong, but I was content. It had been a good day. An exhausting day. A day that brought some closure to this unexpected chapter in my life.

◆ ◆ ◆

By the end of December, one year after the night my world went flat, I was once again teaching my sage-ing classes at The Towers. I also accepted the occasional consulting assignment when it came my way, as I was no longer wedded to the belief that only a job that allowed me to express the ideas of the Work could support my spiritual practice. Yet, while I could do all the things I used to do, I no longer wanted to. I had heard the whisper of death in the wind and my priorities had shifted. The future no longer stretched out before me like an infinite highway vanishing into the horizon. *Gam ki eilech bigeh tzalmavet.* I had been walking in the valley overshadowed by death since my very first breath. This truth became the ever-present reality for me.

I was no longer interested in a life writ large. I was not doing anything to drum up new regulatory business or venues for my programs. Most days, my good-bye to Andy in the morning was the last word I spoke until he returned at night. I had a lot of time to review my life, where I had been and where I was going. It was in doing less and reflecting more that my life was taking on a greater fullness. There was, of course, the everyday business of living to tend to—preparing meals, cleaning house, paying bills—but I was determined to remain disengaged from nonessential busy-ness. Too much was at stake. I was far from where I wanted to be as a human being. I had a lot of growing to do and there was only a small window open in time in which to get it done. That window was closing.

Still, though I affirmed again and again that I was no longer after success and recognition, there was that damn cast of characters to contend with. They were not, one and all, on board with my commitment to put the Work first. Profound insights, one moment razor sharp and clear as crystal, could be obscured by an impenetrable haze in the next. I had to keep reminding myself of the urgency of the situation. I didn't believe in a heaven or a hell. I didn't concern myself with the afterlife. I wanted to know God and as far as I was concerned, I had one shot at it, and this was it.